RECORDS

OF

CAPTAIN CLAPPERTON'S

LAST EXPEDITION.

VOL. I.　　　　A

Drawn by W.Bagg, Jun. Engraved by T.A.Dean.

RICHARD LANDER.

RECORDS

OF

CAPTAIN CLAPPERTON'S

LAST EXPEDITION

TO

AFRICA:

By RICHARD LANDER,

HIS FAITHFUL ATTENDANT, AND THE ONLY SURVIVING
MEMBER OF THE EXPEDITION:

WITH THE
SUBSEQUENT ADVENTURES OF THE AUTHOR.

IN TWO VOLUMES.

VOL. I.

Rediscovery Books

Reproduced by kind permission of the
Royal Geographical Society

Published by
Rediscovery Books Ltd
Unit 10, Ridgewood Industrial Park,
Uckfield, East Sussex,
TN22 5QE England
Tel: +44 (0) 1825 749494
Fax: +44 (0) 1825 765701

This edition © Rediscovery Books Ltd 2006

To find out more about Rediscovery Books
and its range of titles visit
www.rediscoverybooks.com

Published in association with

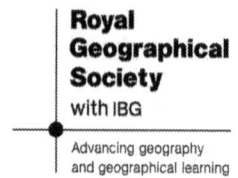

The **Royal Geographical Society with IBG** was founded in 1830 to advance geographical science. Today it supports geographical research, promotes geography in schools and through outdoor learning, in society and to policy makers. Geography connects us to the world's people, places and environments.
The **Rediscovery Books** series allow us to see how previous geographers and travellers understood and recorded the world.

In reprinting in facsimile from the original, any imperfections are inevitably reproduced and the quality may fall short of modern type and cartographic standards.

Printed and bound by Lightning Source

CONTENTS

OF THE FIRST VOLUME.

	Page
INTRODUCTION	ix
SKETCH OF THE AUTHOR'S LIFE . . .	1

CHAPTER I.

List of the Gentlemen and others engaged in the Mission — The Brazen sails from Portsmouth — Touches at the Madeiras, Canaries, and Cape de Verd Islands — Pursues and overtakes a French slave ship — Falls in with H. M. S. Swinger — Arrives and anchors at Sierra Leone — The Author's first illness 15

CHAPTER II.

The ship sails again—Captures a Spanish schooner with slaves—The natives on the coast come on board—Vessel anchors at Cape Coast—Sails from thence, and captures another slave vessel—Arrives at Whydah, where Mr. Dickson lands—His progress through the country, and reported death—The Brazen comes to an anchor in Badagry Roads—The Gentlemen of the Mission give a last farewell to the officers on board, and proceed on shore 29

CHAPTER III.

The travellers reach Badagry, and leave that city on the 7th of December—Dr. Morrison's illness—Arrival at Latoo—Captain Pearce and the Author attacked with fever—Enter Jannah—Continued and alarming illness of the party—Their progress—Dr. Morrison returns to Jannah . 45

CHAPTER IV.

Deaths of Dawson, Captain Pearce, and Dr. Morrison—Their funeral—The survivors, after meeting with various occurrences, and experiencing the kindest hospitality from the natives on their route, arrive at Katunga, the capital of Yariba, on the 15th of January, 1826 73

CHAPTER V.

Residence at Katunga—Ebo the Eunuch—Pantomimic representation by the Yaribeans—Departure from the city of Katunga—Arrival at Khiama—Wow Wow—Manners of the People—Boussa—Mungo Park 108

CHAPTER VI.

Widow Zuma's Love Adventures—Departure from Wow Wow—Arrival at Coulfo—Civil war in Nyffé—Ceremonies observed by the people of Coulfo at the end of the Rhamadan—Tornado at that place, and its disastrous consequences—The Travellers quit Coulfo, and proceed on their journey—The Author attacked with dysentery—His sufferings—Noble conduct of Captain Clapperton towards him—They enter Zeg Zeg—Arrive at Kano 150

CHAPTER VII.

Residence at Kano—Captain Clapperton leaves for Soccatoo—History of Pasko, the Houssa Interpreter—Pasko's robberies and confinement—Return of the Captain with the Godado, after an ineffectual attempt to reach Soccatoo—His second departure from Kano—His Letters 198

CONTENTS.

CHAPTER VIII.

Page

The Author quits Kano to join his Master—His illness on the road—Anecdotes of the Natives, and his reception by them—Pasko's new robbery, and elopement—He is overtaken, and brought back—The Tuarick merchants—The Author's arrival at Soccatoo, the metropolis of the Falatah empire—Residence there—Pasko's dismissal, conduct, and marriage 231

CHAPTER IX.

Religion—Laws—Government—Amusements, &c. of the Natives from Badagry to Soccatoo—Slavery in the interior countries—Timidity of the people—State of the Arts amongst them—Dry and Wet Seasons 270

INTRODUCTION.

On my return from Africa in the summer of 1828, I was so ill with fever and debility, that I had neither spirit nor inclination to devote much time to the compilation and arrangement of my notes, and of the short sketches of character taken by stealth in the heart of that continent. My duty and sole design, in laying my Journal before the British Government, were to satisfy Ministers with regard to my conduct after the decease of Captain Clapperton, my lamented master; and to make them acquainted with the manner in which the property left in my charge at Soccatoo had been disposed of, in my hazardous journey back to the sea-coast. Besides, I had not seen my friends in Cornwall for a period little short of thirteen years; and it is quite natural to suppose that I should have felt a longing to re-visit the place of my nativity, after so protracted and painful an absence. It is not to be wondered at, when all this is considered, that my printed Narrative, drawn up in haste, and without having received the benefit of even the slightest assistance, except from a younger brother, should be incomplete, and in many instances carelessly expressed.

To remedy, if possible, these defects, and to insert the relation of a thousand amusing incidents which had been overlooked, I have in the following pages given my Narrative a new and a more complete dress; and I sincerely hope that my countrymen will not be displeased at my humble but persevering attempts to depict, in true colours, the customs and ceremonies of the powerful nations or tribes inhabiting that vast tract of country lying between Badagry and the beautiful kingdom of Houssa.

The natives of the regions traversed by Captain Clapperton and myself ever regarded our writing apparatus with mingled sensations of alarm and jealousy; and fancied, when they observed us using them, that we were making *fetishes* (charms) and enchantments prejudicial to their lives and interests. To this cause is attributable the absence of many particulars, both in my master's Journal and my own, which, though unimportant in themselves, serve to pourtray, and to place in a natural and lively point of view, the most conspicuous touches in the character of the African, and gradually to develope his passions, prejudices, and remarkable superstitions. We were unwilling to raise up enemies against us in a strange land, by continuing, in presence of the people, a practice which awakened their jealousy, and served only to make us objects of distrust and hatred to them all. Hence we were obliged to cherish in our memory various particulars which we were unable, at that period, to put on paper; contenting ourselves with the hope that, on our return to England, we should have ample leisure to devote to the accomplishment of that object; this was, however, unfortunately frustrated by the decease of Captain Clapperton. I myself have consequently taken the liberty, in the following pages, of attempting to carry into execution the project which that intrepid officer had in view—when alive, and in the full hope of returning to his native land.

The recreations and songs of the people, as well as their wars, laws, religion and government, I have endeavoured faithfully to describe. Of course it cannot be expected that a person in my humble situation of life should have powers of language sufficient to give these descriptions the fullest charm of which they may be susceptible: yet I have done the best my poor abilities would allow me. I have translated several songs from the figurative language of the natives into the English tongue, adopting the similes, and copying the mode of expression, as nearly as the idiom of the former would permit; while, in the absence of technical terms relative to law, &c., I have chosen words which have appeared to me the simplest, and which indeed occur most easily to me.

The engagements of the Falatahs with their sable neighbours can scarcely fail of being inter-

INTRODUCTION.   xiii

esting in many points of view; and their manner of making war is characteristic of African customs. That aggrandizing power, like the government of Russia in Europe, is making rapid and gigantic strides towards an enormous despotism; and should it hereafter possess so martial and enterprising a ruler as its founder, Dandfodio, in the course of a very few years the whole of Central and Northern, if not of Western Africa, will be under the *surveillance* of the restless Falatah; and the worship of snakes and idols be supplanted by the fanatical tenets of Islamism.

The history of the far-famed Borghoo-Arabian lady, widow Zuma, is correct in every particular; the elopement of that most bulky individual will, it is trusted, be found amusing in the extreme; and the whole train of her adventures—her passionate fondness for white men—the marvel of her extraordinary plumpness—her excessive hospitality—the splendour of her retinue and domestic establishment—her inordinate ambition in attempting to dethrone her lawful sovereign, the innocent and facetious Mohammed—her mournful reverse of fortune—

her confinement—the song of her maidens—and her last request,—are singularly remarkable, and strongly pourtray the disposition and habits of an eminent African belle.

The narrative of Pasko, or rather, I should say, of *Abbu Becr*, our Houssa interpreter, contrasted with that of the amiable and accomplished Zuma, will not be found to be altogether destitute of attraction, insomuch as it shows the manners and superstitions of his countrymen much more pleasingly than a laboured description of them would do; while the archness, drollery, and dishonesty of the old scoundrel, together with his warm and deep attachment to the gentler sex, and his entire devotedness to their service, are accurately related, as the circumstances which called those various passions into action took place.

After the decease of Captain Pearce and Dr. Morrison, when my late valued master and myself were the only Europeans left of the mission, Captain Clapperton for various reasons thought proper to style me his son, and the natives ever after regarded that gallant officer as my father.

Surrounded as we were by strange faces and strange scenes, cut off from all communication with civilized society, and wandering, far from our native country, and all that was truly dear to us, in barbarous regions, and oftentimes through long dismal woods, and awful solitudes; we became linked to each other by the strongest of all ties. Ours, if I may so express myself, were kindred spirits; we entered into each other's views, shared each other's gladness and melancholy, hope and despair, and participated in each other's feelings and amusements. It was for the interest of both to do so. It would not have been well for any haughtiness or reserve to be manifested towards me under such circumstances, merely because accident had thrown me into a lower rank in life than my master; and it would have been unfeeling, nay unmanly, when bowed down by pain and wretchedness in the heart of Africa, for a British officer to refuse, for no other reason, to the humble companion of his wanderings that confidence and friendship which he had in some measure a right to expect. Such, happily, was not the disposition of Captain Clapperton; the difference in our respective conditions was willingly levelled, as it certainly ought to have been, by that gentleman; and for my part I may justly say, that my attachment for him was so great that I would cheerfully have undergone any privation rather than that he should have been a sufferer; or, if necessity required it, would even have laid down my life with pleasure for the preservation of his.

To Capt. Clapperton I owe the existence I enjoy at the present moment; and for him I would have sacrificed, and perhaps I *did* sacrifice on particular occasions, every consideration of personal comfort or convenience. To " smooth down his lonely pillow;" to mingle my hopes, and fears, and distresses, with his; and to render the transition from life to eternity as easy as possible, were my employments when the unfortunate Captain was stretched out upon his death-bed, in a dismal solitary hut in Soccatoo; and these services themselves, Heaven knows, carried their own reward along with them. The affectionate grasp of the hand—the

INTRODUCTION. xvii

trembling eye — the *look* of approbation and thankfulness—expressed more eloquently and feelingly than words could have done the gratitude of my heroic master and preserver for my humble endeavours to serve him, when his cup of pain, disappointment, and sorrow, was foaming to the brim; and the readers of my "Wanderings" will excuse me for dwelling on this subject in the chapter devoted to the illness and decease of Capt. Clapperton, &c. At this distance of time and place even, I reflect on that gloomy and distressing period with emotion; I recall to my remembrance all that passed there—disease, suffering, loneliness, and death; yet do I often wish that my latter end may be as gentle as was my master's; more calm I do not expect it to be—less free from pain it cannot be.

After all that I have said on this subject, the charge of having assumed too much consequence in speaking so familiarly of Capt. Clapperton, will not surely be brought against me; yet in conversation I have heard it asserted that this sin was committed in my printed journal; but the remark needs no refutation. I have not chosen to alter this imputed consequence in the following narrative, simply because there is no apparent necessity for doing so; and in this opinion the generality of my countrymen will, I am confident, agree with me.

My description of the savage manners and horrid barbarities of the people of Badagry, at the celebration of their monthly sacrifices, &c. is by no means exaggerated. At present these seem unknown to Englishmen; and my reasons for not relating them before are already given. I had no intention of having my Journal printed, and therefore did not study to render the perusal of it interesting by inserting in it observations that did not come strictly within the compass of the plan which I had originally laid down for myself.

In the composition of the following pages I must acknowledge my obligations to a younger brother, and (with the exception of the customary revision of the printed sheets) to him alone. I should feel both pleasure and pride in expressing, in this place, my gratitude for even a hint received from any other quarter; but as this has not, even in a solitary instance, been the case, I have no such thanks to offer. Although unused to composition, my brother devoted, during the past summer, the little leisure which relaxation from his daily labour afforded him, to the office of copying my notes and observations, and putting them into something like arrangement. Having become impressed with my thoughts, he has "turned them to shape," and, entering warmly into my feelings, he has depicted my emotions, even as I felt them; and the public will best discern whether they are true to nature or not.

I beg to introduce this little Work to the notice of my countrymen with the greatest humility. They will not judge of it by too severe a standard; they will not — I am sure they will not—accuse me of presumption in my feeble attempts to portray the manners and peculiarities of a strange people. I have done the utmost to render the perusal of my Narrative agreeable; and to give the reader a correct idea of the state of society in the interior of Africa. It were unreasonable to expect that my limited knowledge should permit me to give a learned or laboured description of regions which had never before been visited by Europeans; yet I repeat 1 have done the best my power would allow; and no one will, I think, feel any disposition to question the truth of this declaration.

THE AUTHOR.

Truro,
October, 1829.

Since the preceding introductory remarks were written, His Majesty's Government have engaged me to proceed to Fundah, and trace the river from thence to Benin; so that before the public will be put in possession of the following Narrative, in all probability, I shall be on my way to the Western Coast of Africa. In this new undertaking I shall be accompanied only by my brother (John Lander), whose assistance in the composition of this work I have already acknowledged; and if energy and perseverance can avail us any thing, I have the best reasons for believing that it will prove as successful as my most sanguine expectations lead me to hope that it will.

At all events, nothing shall be wanting on our parts to accomplish the object in view. If we be so unfortunate as to fail in the object, I may say with confidence and without vanity, that it shall not be attributed to a want of proper spirit and enterprise; since we have made the fixed determination to risk every thing, even life itself, towards its final accomplishment. We shall endeavour to conform ourselves, as nearly as possible, to the manners and habits of the natives; we will not mock their blind superstition, but respect it; we will not scoff at their institutions, but bow to them; we will not condemn their prejudices, but pity them. In fine, we shall do all in our power to ward off suspicion as to the integrity of our motives, and the innocency of our intentions; and this cannot be done more effectually than by mingling with the people in their general amusements and diversions. Confidence in ourselves, and in them, will be our best panoply; and an English Testament our safest *fetish*. Clothed in *this* armour, by the blessing of God, we have not much to fear; but if, by any casualty or unforeseen misfortune, we perish in Africa, and are seen no more, even then our fate will not be more dismal than that of many of our predecessors in the same pursuit, whose gallant enterprising spirits have sunk into darkness, without a voice to record their melancholy end. If *this* should be our case, our countrymen may, perhaps, be moved to respect our memory; and, at all events, it is some consolation to know that the gap we may make in society will scarcely be observed at all; or, if observed, soon filled up:

"For we to the world are like a drop of water
That in the ocean falls."

London,
Dec. 1829.

LIST OF ILLUSTRATIONS.

Portrait of Richard Lander	Frontispiece.
Pelicans feeding their young	vol. II. p. 16
Funeral of Captain Clapperton	78
Fainting Scene	93
Crossing the streams at Yariba	215
Heads of Natives with Tattoo marks	218
Ordeal by Poison	257

ERRATA.

Page 89, for Kang read *Kong*.
Page 156, omit the preposition "*to*" after "lead me."
From p. 134 to p. 269, for Soecasoo read *Soccatoo*.
At the head of chap. II. p. 29, for Cape Coast read *Papoe*.

SKETCH

OF THE

AUTHOR'S LIFE.

MANY allusions to my earlier history occurring in the following pages, it may not, perhaps, be deemed impertinent on my part, if I should attempt to give a short and hasty sketch of my life, devoted as it has been to perpetual wandering, and chequered by a thousand misfortunes.

My family is as ancient, I dare say, as that of any upon the face of the earth, although, notwithstanding the profoundest research, I have been unable to trace its descent, with genealogical accuracy and precision, to a more remote era than the period of my grandfather's nonage; the history of all my ancestors previous to him, being either mixed with fable, or involved in doubt and uncertainty. If the ancient saying of the people of Cornwall, that,

> " By Tre, Pol, *Lan,* and *Pen,*
> You may know most Cornishmen,"

be entitled to credit, then undoubtedly my family is of pure Cornish extraction; and I would respectfully suggest that it has a double claim, in the present generation, to the enviable distinction of antiquity, my mother's maiden name being *Pen*-rose, and my father's name *Lan*-der. Thus much for my pedigree; and I have the solitary satisfaction of boasting of at least one celebrated character in its humble records, my grandfather, by my mother's side, who was a noted wrestler in his day, and lived some fifty years since near the Land's End.

I am the fourth of six children, and was born at Truro, in Cornwall, in 1804, on the very day on which Colonel Lemon was elected Member of Parliament for the Borough. Owing to this striking coincidence, singular as it may seem, my father, who was fond of sounding appellations, at the simple suggestion of the doctor who attended the family, added *Lemon* to my baptismal name of Richard: an example of the trivial means by which people are oftentimes accommodated with an extra name. As nothing remarkable occurred for the first five or six years after I came into the world, I shall pass them over in silence, simply observing, that when yet in infancy, whilst I was in the act of gazing one morning at something attached to the ceiling of my father's stable, a piece of iron, having a sharpened edge, fell and entered my forehead; which accident was of so serious a nature that I was ill for several weeks, and narrowly escaped with life.

My rambling inclinations began to display themselves in early youth. I was never easy a great while together in one place, and used to be delighted to play truant and stroll from town to town, and from village to village, whenever I could steal an opportunity as well; as to mix in the society of boys possessing restless habits and inclinations similar to my own. I used also to listen with unmixed attention to old women's tales about the manners and ceremonies of the natives of distant regions of the earth, and never felt greater pleasure than when, dangling me on their knees, or stroking down my face with their aged hands, they used to say, " you will be sure to see two kingdoms, Richard, for you have two *crowns upon your head!* " Their marvellous descriptions of monsters existing, they affirmed, in remote lands, likewise conspired to raise in me a longing to be a traveller; for the venerable matrons of my native county, moving in the humbler walks of life, like those of most other counties and nations, are fond of the wonderful, and endeavour to stamp a love of it in the tender mind of youth with all the solemnity and earnestness of age and belief. These tales, how incredible soever they might have been, made a deep and permanent impression on my thoughts; and though so very young, I formed a resolution, or rather felt a strong and violent inclination to become a wanderer, in order that the story of *my* adventures might one day rival in interest those to which I had listened with so devout an attention; perhaps also a childish feeling of pride entered my bosom as I used to say to myself: " And when I shall have returned from such and such a place, and seen all the strange sights in them, my former companions will look upon me with a mixture of wonder and admiration, and I shall excite the envy of the other boys."

Thus the first period of my life flew swiftly away; and I was no more than nine years of age, as nearly as my memory, at this distance of time, will allow me to guess, when owing to a series of domestic misfortunes, which it would be a tedious and unpleasant task here to particularise, I left the paternal roof, and have ever since been almost a stranger in the place of my nativity.

The frequent observation of my lamented mother, " Remember, my poor child, the old proverb, 'a rolling stone gathers no moss,'" has been entirely thrown away upon me, for between necessity and choice I have ever been in motion; and with respect to "*moss*," taken in its figurative signification, I have certainly, in my own person, verified the truth of the homely adage above alluded to, scarcely ever having been able to retain a single handful in my grasp for any length of time together.

At the early age of eleven years I accompanied a mercantile gentleman to the West Indies, and whilst in St. Domingo was attacked with the fever of the country, suffering so severely under its influence that my life was despaired of; but, owing chiefly to the kindness and attention I experienced from some benevolent and sympathizing Negro females, joined to my youth and a naturally vigorous constitution, I recovered my wonted health, and after an absence of three years returned to my native country in 1818. From that period till the attainment of my 19th year, I lived in the service of various noblemen and gentlemen, one of whom I accompanied to France, and other countries on the Continent; when, hearing on my return to London, that Major Colebrook, one of His Majesty's Commissioners of Inquiry into the

State of the British Colonies, was in want of an individual to proceed with him in the capacity of servant, I quitted the office I then held, and procured the vacant situation with little difficulty. With this gentleman I embarked from Portsmouth on board the Lady Campbell, which weighed anchor on the thirteenth of February, 1823, and after a stormy and hazardous voyage of nearly five months, arrived in Simmons's Bay, South Africa, on the 13th of July following. During the passage our unfortunate vessel, in which were upwards of forty ladies and gentlemen (passengers) with twenty servants, very nearly escaped destruction no less than three times. In the first instance, she encountered a heavy gale on the 8th of March, in which she lost her rudder, and leaked four feet of water in the hold. After being buffeted about by the wind and waves for four or five days, her distressed condition was observed by a small French brig belonging to L'Orient, which towed her into that port. There she was laid up for six weeks, in order that the serious damage she had sustained might be repaired;

when, on the 1st of May, she again set sail. On the 10th of June following, a lady, passing near the gun-room, discovered it to be on fire, and immediately gave the alarm. After incredible exertions, and still greater noise, hurry, bustle, and confusion, the progress of the flames was arrested, and the fire finally extinguished, to the no small gratification of every one on board, who feared, and with justice, that from the proximity of the gun-room to the powder-magazine the most imminent danger was to be apprehended. This was not the last fright we experienced, for on the night of entering Simmons's Bay the vessel unfortunately struck on a rock called by seamen "The Noah's Ark," but was happily lifted by the swell of the sea from her perilous situation, without being materially damaged by the shock; and nothing worthy of notice occurred till her arrival before Cape Town, Cape of Good Hope, as above mentioned.

After accompanying Major Colebrook in his journeyings from one extremity of that important colony to the other,—for a reason which it would be superfluous in this place to adduce,

I left his service, and sailing from Cape Town, arrived in England in 1824. I had not been many weeks in the metropolis before I accepted of a situation in the establishment of a kinsman to the Duke of Northumberland, where my time passed away pleasantly and thoughtlessly enough; till the return of Captain Clapperton and Major Denham from the interior of Africa, in the following year, again aroused my rambling propensities, and I could not help reproaching myself for having remained so long a time in a state of comparative indolence. Determined from that hour to embrace the first favourable chance of once more quitting my native shores, to whichever part of the globe fate or fortune might destine me, I waited impatiently for something to take place in furtherance of the object I had most at heart; and an opportunity soon offered itself that promised to gratify my fondest and warmest inclinations, as well as amply to satisfy the inordinate desire I could not suppress of visiting foreign countries.

Having heard that it was the intention of the British Government to send out another expedition for the purpose of exploring the yet undiscovered parts of central Africa, and of endeavouring to ascertain the source, progress, and termination, of the myterious Niger; and the attempt coinciding exactly with my long-cherished wishes, I instantly waited upon the late Captain Clapperton, who I was told was to be placed at its head, and expressed to that brave and spirited officer the great eagerness I felt to become a party, however humble, to the novel and hazardous undertaking into which he was about to enter. The Captain listened to me with attention, and after I had answered a few interrogations, willingly engaged me to be his confidential servant. In this interview the keen, penetrating eye of the African traveller, did not escape my observation; and by its fire, energy, and quickness, denoted, in my own opinion at least, the very soul of enterprize and adventure.

Having made the necessary arrangements, I entered with a light heart upon my new duties, and enjoyed the thoughts of following the bias of my own inclination with as great a zest as if the path of my future life had been strewed with flowers.

I had not, however, adopted this line of conduct without deep reflection on the difficulties that would, in all probability, accompany it. The destruction that had overwhelmed former travellers, engaged in the same pursuit, was by no means unfamiliar to me; and the melancholy story of Mungo Park and his companions in misfortune, in particular, had often crossed my thoughts. I felt a degree of shuddering sympathy for those enterprizing individuals, (heightened perhaps by the cloud of darkness in which their latter end was shrouded,) which no fictitious tale of woe had been ever able to excite in my bosom; yet even this failed in staggering my resolution, or overcoming my early and deeply-rooted prejudices.

There was a charm in the very sound of Africa, that always made my heart flutter on hearing it mentioned: whilst its boundless deserts of sand; the awful obscurity in which many of the interior regions were enveloped; the strange and wild aspect of countries that had never been trodden by the foot of a European, and even the very failure of all former undertakings to explore its hidden wonders, united to strengthen the determination I had come to, of embracing the earliest opportunity of penetrating into the interior of that immense Continent.

In vain my London acquaintances urged upon me the risk 1 should incur of finding a grave in Africa; and equally vain were the kind representations of a medical gentleman of the metropolis, who painted to me in lively colours the imminent danger to which my life would be exposed, by reason of my youth, inexperience, and habit of body. I disregarded all the counsel that the world could give me, and perhaps secretly depended on the strength of an unimpaired constitution to support me in sickness, and bring me out of every difficulty; so prone are we to indulge the belief that there is a something different, a latent excellence within us, which does not belong to the persons or characters of the rest of the world; and so just is the observation of the poet, that

" All men think all men mortal but themselves."

As soon as my relatives in Cornwall were made acquainted with the step I was about to take, they expressed the deepest concern and sorrow, and sent me numbers of letters, couched in the simple and affectionate language of nature, expressive of their feelings, and endeavouring to dissuade me from proceeding to a region they all so greatly and justly dreaded. George Croker Fox, Esq. a highly respectable gentleman, residing at Grove Hill, near Falmouth, with the spirit of amiable benevolence by which he is so peculiarly distinguished, also exerted himself in the same object, promising that if my determination to leave England was fixed, rather than that I should expose myself to the dangers to be apprehended from African exploration, he would procure me a more lucrative situation in one of the South American republics. But no inducement under the sun could make me swerve, even in thought, from the line of duty I had laid down for myself; or cool the ardour that warned me to attempt, at least, the accomplishment of the great object towards which my earliest thoughts had been intently directed. Indeed, I had already gone too far to recede; and leaving the metropolis with Captain Clapperton, I arrived at Portsmouth, in order to embark in the Brazen sloop of war, Captain Willis, on the 24th of August, 1825, being then in the 21st year of my age.

WANDERINGS
IN
AFRICA.

CHAPTER I.

List of the Gentlemen and others engaged in the Mission—The Brazen sails from Portsmouth—Touches at the Madeiras, Canaries, and Cape de Verd Islands—Pursues and overtakes a French slave ship—Falls in with H. M. S. Swinger—Arrives and anchors at Sierra Leone—The Author's first illness.

ON arriving at Portsmouth with Captain Clapperton, I found the following gentlemen, his associates in the mission, waiting for him:—Captain Pearce, R. N. an amiable individual, but whose frame was much too delicate for the arduous task he had undertaken; Dr. Morrison, a navy surgeon; and Dr. Dickson, a Scotchman, who had served as a surgeon for a long period in the West Indies. These were attended by Columbus, a West Indian mulatto, who had accompanied Major Denham in the previous journey; Pasko, a black, native of Haussa; and myself.

We embarked on the 27th of August, 1825; and, a light breeze springing up from the northeast, the vessel got under weigh and made sail, the shores of England gradually lessening from our view. After touching at Porto Santo, the least of the Madeiras, on the 8th September, where the Gentlemen of the Mission landed and obtained various specimens of plants and minerals, the vessel dropped anchor at Santa Cruz, Teneriffe, on the 13th of the same month. Next day, Captain Clapperton and his coadjutors, accompanied by three officers of the Brazen, went on shore to make an excursion to the Peak; but my master being taken suddenly unwell on the road from Santa Cruz, was obliged to remain at Oratavia, a fine but irregularly built town, situated at the base of a cluster of mountains, out of which rises the celebrated Peak, from which it is distant about four or five miles. The travellers having accomplished the object of their jaunt, came back with minerals, &c. complaining sadly of fatigue. On the 16th, we returned to Santa Cruz, the rugged nature of the roads, together with the stubborn disposition of the asses with which we were accommodated, being in great measure overlooked by the mirthful humour and innocent jocularity of our native guides, who enlivened us by singing and playing on guitars nearly the whole of the way to the capital, frequently interrupting themselves by shouting "Long live the English!" The inhabitants were mostly employed in gathering in the grapes, with which the island abounds; and we were met on the road by great numbers of them with mules and asses loaded with this delicious fruit, returning to their respective habitations.

On the 16th the Brazen again set sail with a fair wind; and on the 24th following arrived at St. Antonia, one of the Cape de Verd islands, where Captain Clapperton landed, as on former occasions, and obtained minerals, &c. from its lofty mountains. The vessel weighed anchor the same evening, and nothing requiring particular observation occurred for several days, the wind continuing tolerably fair, but squally.

On the 4th of October, a small schooner came in sight, and supposing she had slaves on board, the Brazen chased and overtook her. She proved, however, to be a Russian merchant vessel, bound for Pernambuco, and was of course suffered to proceed on her voyage as soon as the error was discovered. On the 8th of the same month another sail was descried, and suspecting also that she was engaged in the nefarious traffic in slaves, we pursued and boarded her. The suspicions were confirmed on discovering 196 human beings in this French schooner (which was bound for St. Domingo) chained together in couples, and literally crammed between decks, which being barely three feet in height the slaves were obliged to remain in a sitting posture whilst they stayed on board. So strong and disagreeable an odour proceeded from the confined place in which these poor creatures were huddled, that the air was tainted with it, and I hastened on board the Brazen as fast as I could; shortly after which the French vessel proceeded with her living cargo to the place of her destination.

On the 19th the Brazen fell in with H.M. ship Swinger, on a cruise. This vessel had lost nineteen men with fever, and was short of provisions and water. After relieving her wants, and sending a doctor on board, we continued our course with a fair light breeze, and on the 21st entered the river of Sierra Leone.

The day after our arrival I went on shore, and sauntered alone through Free Town, visiting the church and other public buildings. I was grieved to see that sacred edifice converted into a market-place, and buyers and sellers indecently disputing and wrangling in the temple of God. The colony was rather sickly, and the great number of deaths which had recently taken place sufficiently attested the extreme unhealthiness of that immense "charnel-house." The country in the neighbourhood of the town is rich and fertile, producing in great abundance many kinds of fruits and vegetables. West Indian, and other tropical productions are cultivated with success, and to a great extent, on the banks of the river. Cattle and poultry, which are of inferior size and description, are excessively scarce and dear; but the inhabitants do not seem to feel much interested in the improvement of the breed of their domestic animals. The grass in the colony, though apparently rich and luxuriant, contains in reality but little nutriment; and to this cause, more than to any other, the sorry condition of the cattle is attributable.

The Kroomen, great numbers of whom reside at Sierra Leone, are a fine athletic people; active, clean, and industrious. They have a village at no great distance from Free Town, which I visited. It consists of a great number of huts, most of which have a little meadow-land, or garden, attached to them; but a very small portion of the soil is cultivated in its vicinity, the male inhabitants being generally employed by the masters of European vessels visiting Sierra

Leone, who find them extremely serviceable. Notwithstanding their intercourse with the English and other European nations, which has been preserved for so long a period, the Kroomen still retain their native costume, which consists simply of a piece of cotton cloth, tied carelessly round the waist, and extending to the knees. Almost the whole of them have obtained a smattering of the English tongue, in which they pride themselves; whilst many of the more intelligent can converse in it with tolerable fluency. Upwards of twenty different languages, it is said, are spoken by the mixed population of the colony, who have been principally captured from the slave vessels of the Portuguese or Spaniards, and have been brought from many of the interior countries.

On the 23d I again went on shore with my gun, to shoot in a savannah at a short distance from the town, in which I remained a great part of the day, amongst high coarse grass and thick jungle, indiscreetly exposing my head to the scorching rays of a vertical sun; in consequence of which I was attacked in the evening with giddiness of the head, and other symptoms of fever; but having been bled copiously, and having taken proper medicine, the progress of the disease was for the time arrested. My illness, which was not particularly severe, was of short duration, and I fondly expected that this was but the *seasoning* every European should be prepared to encounter on visiting tropical countries.

Having taken in her supplies of fresh water and provisions, the Brazen got under weigh on the 27th of October, and made sail for Cape Coast, with a fresh breeze from the south-east. On the following day a thunder-storm arose, accompanied by heavy and continued rain and vivid flashes of lightning, which lasted for several hours; and on the 2d of November a sail being perceived at some distance, the ship gave her chase, and on coming up with her, she proved to be the Fortune, a Spanish schooner, with thirty-five slaves only on board, not having then received her full complement. The vessel was immediately captured, and sent back to Sierra Leone. Next day another sail was discovered, and being overtaken, was found to be a French brig from Martinique, waiting for a cargo of human beings.

On the 5th the natives came out to meet the Brazen in canoes, with yams, plantains, bananas, cassada, and other productions of the country, which they bartered for tobacco, that article being in great request with them. Their canoes were lightly and ingeniously constructed, and propelled through the water with singular swiftness and dexterity, the rowers performing their laborious task in a kneeling posture. They were completely destitute of clothing of any kind.

On the 7th we were honored with a visit from the Kroo king, who is a jet black of goodly stature, and of simple but prepossessing manners. On his head the sable monarch had a European hat, and across his loins was fastened a plain piece of cotton cloth purchased from the English. He wore a necklace of *gris-gris* (charms or amulets) made of leather, in the merits of which he seemed to repose implicit confidence, believing himself the most fortunate of men in having it in his possession; and as long as that was the case, he asserted, neither demon nor human being could in any wise injure him.

One of his majesty's attendants, as blindly superstitious as his sovereign, to put the virtues of *his* amulet to the test, entreated me several times to discharge a musket loaded with ball at him, at the distance of only a few yards, which, when I refused to do, he appeared to be considerably chagrined and disappointed, and went away muttering that the English were the most uncivil people in the world.

The following day, although the ship was at the distance of several miles from the shore, others of the natives came alongside, differing but little in external appearance from their neighbours who had visited us on the former occasions: but in addition to their other ornaments, they wore iron rings round the neck, with little bells of the same metal appended, which, on the slightest movement of the wearer, made a jingling noise not unlike bells hung to the necks of waggon-horses in England. The

Cape Palmas king, accompanied by a great number of his subjects, also condescended to come on board on the 9th. He is a powerful athletic man, having a bold expression of countenance, but of gentle and social habits, and he was graciously pleased to converse freely with any one on deck, who felt disposed, or had patience enough to listen to his remarks.

There was this peculiarity in the appearance of his majesty's followers: their heads were shaved either partially or wholly, and the hair of those that had any being cut into a thousand fantastic modes and forms, looked exceedingly grotesque. Many of the tribes on the coast, indeed, appear to devote a large portion of their time to dressing and ornamenting their hair, which in some districts is plaited and braided with much care, and peculiar taste and neatness. Others friz out the hair like the natives of the Tonga islands, and as it is anointed with a species of red clay, softened with palm-oil, which is found in great abundance on the coast, it adds greatly to the ferocity of their appearance.

The Brazen continued her course with a

tolerably fair wind but heavy showers, and having passed several towns and villages, the inhabitants of some of which occasionally visited her in canoes, arrived at Cape Coast on the 14th, at one p.m.

Cape Coast castle is a strongly-built stone fortification, capable of containing within its walls the whole of the population of the town it defends; the habitations of which are constructed in much the same style as those with which the whole line of coast is thickly studded; being built of earth, and thatched with rushes, interlaced with palm-leaves.

A great number of people have settled in the town from the interior countries; but by far the major part of the inhabitants are Fantees, who have voluntarily placed themselves under the protection of the British fortress, in order the more effectually to secure to themselves the blessings of peace, and preserve their property from the rapacity of their more restless countrymen, and the neighbouring nations.

Cleanliness is by no means a characteristic of the Fantees at Cape Coast, animal and vegetable substances being allowed to accumulate and putrify in the streets, from which is exhaled so noxious an effluvium, that the air, impregnated with it, is rendered extremely insalubrious, particularly to Europeans.

It is perhaps a fortunate circumstance, that vultures, attracted by the intolerable odour, resort thither in vast numbers, voraciously devouring the filth which the indolent inhabitants are either too lazy or too *ignorant* to remove; for they cannot be persuaded that disease of any kind is engendered by such means. If this had not been the case, it would be a miracle indeed that Europeans should exist in the town many weeks; and even the Africans themselves, in all likelihood, would speedily fall victims to pestilential disorders.

Horned cattle are not less scarce, and yet more diminutive, than at Sierra Leone, and their flesh is of the worst possible quality. Horses, for some reason, are no where to be found on the Gold Coast, nor are any beasts of burden whatever to be met with in the neighbourhood of the Castle; loads of every description being carried on men's heads, and in hammocks fastened to long poles, which are borne by two persons.

The market is rather scantily supplied with Guinea-corn, maize, yams, sweet cassada, &c. although the soil is amazingly rich, yielding abundantly all the necessaries of life. Notwithstanding its fertility, however, cultivation is carried on to a very inconsiderable extent, and the surrounding country is still thickly wooded.

CHAPTER II.

The ship sails again—Capture of a Spanish schooner with Slaves—The natives of the coast come on board—Vessel anchors at Cape Coast—Sails from thence and captures another slave vessel—Arrives at Whydah, where Mr. Dickson lands—His progress through the country and reported death—The Brazen comes to an anchor in Badagry Roads—The Gentlemen of the Mission give a last farewell to the officers on board, and proceed on shore.

THE Brazen sailed from Cape Coast on the 17th, and on the following day pursued a fine Spanish brigantine, which was waiting to receive a cargo of slaves from the coast. After a short chase the vessel was captured, and taken to Accra the same evening. There were only five or six Europeans at Accra; but the town, as at Cape Coast, is chiefly inhabited by Fantees, and is very populous. We had an opportunity of seeing the king of the Fantee nation during our short stay. His majesty, dressed in a shabby uniform of an English military officer, was supported on the shoulders of four men, and paraded through the town, preceded and followed by a number of people, who, by clapping of hands, and beating on *tom-toms!* created a loud and most discordant noise, which might have been heard at a considerable distance from the spot.

On the 20th the Brazen departed with her prize from Accra, and came to an anchor at Papoe the day after. From that place the brigantine was to have taken in her cargo, and the slaves selected were confined in the town. As soon as the officers landed from the ship, they were demanded, but the king, obstinately refusing at first to deliver them up, was told that unless they were immediately produced, his town would be cannonaded, he himself and his son taken prisoners, and the slaves seized by main force; on which the royal personage seemed to pay a little more respect to the imperious summons of the Englishmen; and the unfortunate people were shortly after ordered to be liberated. These slaves at length made their appearance, and exhibited a long line of melancholy faces and emaciated frames, wasted by disease and close confinement, and by having suffered dreadfully from scantiness of food, and the impure air of their prison-house. They were 231 in number, men, women, and children, in a complete state of nudity, and heavily manacled; several of them were lamed by the weight of their irons, and their skin sadly excoriated from the same cause. All of them appeared in the deepest misery, and one little boy in particular was greatly distressed, and cried much and bitterly. He had been seized whilst at play with his young companions from before the threshhold of his parents' hut, and immediately driven to Papoe with his thoughtless playmates. The poor things evinced the liveliest joy on being made acquainted with the favorable turn in their affairs, and the gratitude they displayed to their deliverers was natural and sincere. Arrangements were speedily made for their accommodation on board the prize; and that vessel, which was to have borne them to perpetual slavery in in a remote region, was employed to convey them to hundreds of their countrymen at Sierra Leone.

Papoe lies close to the sea, and consists of an assemblage of irregularly-built mud huts; a number of lofty cocoa-trees growing in its immediate vicinity conducing greatly to the apparent freshness and pleasantness of the place. Slavery is carried on to an alarming extent by the inhabitants, every one of whom is at all times prepared to accompany a slave expedition. They are said to be more ferocious in their manners than most tribes on the coast; and if one may be allowed to judge from the savage expression of their countenances, the people are eminently entitled to this character. The aspect of the country presents the same unvaried uniformity of thick forests and extensive savannas, intersected with rich plains, that is everywhere observable from the sea.

The brigantine haing been sent to Sierra Leone with the emancipated slaves, the Brazen sailed from Papoe on the morning of the 23d, and arrived at Whydah the same evening. Seven sail were at anchor off the coast fronting the town, the greater part of which were supposed to be waiting for a favourable opportunity to embark slaves. Captain Clapperton and Dr. Morrison landed on the following morning, and were conveyed in hammocks to the town of Whydah, situated about two English miles from the beach. After making observations, and obtaining the information they sought, the gentlemen returned the same evening to the ship.

On the 25th Dr. Dickson landed to proceed into the interior. The parting interview between Capt. Clapperton and the warm-hearted Doctor was singularly tender and pathetic. The latter gentleman entertained a presentiment that they should never meet again, and his endeavours to suppress or disguise his emotion entirely failed in their effect. " Study the character of the natives well," said the Captain to Dr. Dickson, as he yet lingered on the deck; "respect their institutions, and be kind to them on all occasions; for 'tis on paying proper respect to these rules, and these only, that you must ground your hope of being successful in your progress through the country; and the conduct of the people to you will be guided solely by your behaviour towards them. Set a guard over your temper, my dear Dickson, and never let it lead you into error." " We meet at Jennah, then," said the Doctor, with an inquiring eye, and anxious, half-doubting look: " We meet at Jennah," answered Captain Clapperton, solemnly. " Once more adieu, my dear Dickson, and may God bless and protect you." The Doctor then tore himself from the deck, and we saw him no more.

Doctor Dickson was met at Whydah by M. de Souza, a Portuguese, and Mr. James, an Englishman, who accompanied him to Abomey, the capital of Dahomy, where he was received both by the king and his subjects with a hearty welcome, and every mark of kindness and respect. He was attacked with fever shortly after his arrival in that metropolis; but on his recovery proceeded in high spirits, with an escort of one hundred men, furnished as a protection by his Dahoman majesty, to Shar, that monarch's authority extending no further in that direction.

DEATH OF DR. DICKSON.

On my return from the interior I was told by a person at Jennah, that Dr. Dickson, having proceeded about two days' journey into the country from Shar, (where he had arrived in safety,) for some reason, which was not correctly explained, had a serious misunderstanding with a party of the natives, and his life being threatened by its chief, he was so violently exasperated that he attempted to throttle that individual; which being observed by his followers, they fell upon the unfortunate doctor, overcame, and slew him.* Thus this gentleman was the first of the mission that fell a victim to the cause of African research.

On the 26th the ship departed from Whydah, and came to an anchor in Badagry Roads on the 28th.

The appearance of the coast from Sierra Leone to Badagry is, generally speaking, singularly beautiful and attractive. The soil differs

---

* Mr. James was attacked with dysentery on his journey to Abomey, but lived to return to Whydah, where he died. It was said that he was assassinated by M. de Souza, but this report was not authenticated.

in various districts, but consists chiefly of a rich reddish mould, intermixed with sand, which renders it wonderfully fertile. It yields in the greatest abundance most, if not all, of the necessaries of life, and many of its luxuries; and millet, Indian corn, yams, sweet potatoes, cassada, plantains, the banana, &c. are cultivated to a considerable extent by the natives. Trees in great number and variety, of magnificent dimensions and luxuriant foliage, adorn the face of the country, the apparent beauty of which is infinitely heightened by the number of small villages, embellished with lovely trees, dotting the borders of the sea; amongst which the stately palm, both on account of the peculiarity and elegance of its form, must ever hold a distinguished place. Thick forests are also spread over the landscape, the gloomy shade of which, contrasted with the smiling verdure of cultivated plains, pleasantly studded with clumps of cocoa and other trees, and enlightened by a brilliant sun, offers a variegated and unrivalled picture of rural beauty, which the eye feasts upon with peculiar pleasure.

It is melancholy to reflect, however, that a great portion of this delightful region is peopled with a race of savages and semi-barbarians, speaking a variety of languages, but all having nearly the same customs, and engaged in perpetual broils amongst each other. The manners and ceremonies of the people are indeed the same, essentially, as they were when the coast was first discovered by the Portuguese in the fifteenth century; neither time, nor their familiar intercourse with Europeans for so many ages, having apparently in the slightest degree either enlightened their minds, or out-rooted their unmeaning superstitions, which still retain all their original freshness and absurdity. It is much to be feared that, instead of copying and imbibing the virtues of their white visitants, they have only adopted their most odious vices. Intoxication, which in all probability was unknown, or at most but partially indulged in, by the aboriginal inhabitants, is followed to a beastly excess at the present time, and is the parent of a thousand irregularities.

Slavery, by far the most appalling evil that

can befal the human race, is carried on in particular districts to a deplorable extent, and spreads like a pestilence through the country. It is impossible to contemplate this striking and peculiar feature in the African habits, without experiencing the most lively emotions of surprise and sorrow. It has insinuated itself so deeply into the very life and spirit of the laws and institutions of the people, that the period seems remote indeed when it may fairly be presumed it will be wholly eradicated from them. It has also produced the most baleful effects, causing anarchy, injustice, and oppression to reign in Africa, and exciting nation to rise up against nation, and man against man; it has damped all ardour for improvement, in the absence of every stimulus to industry and exertion, and infinitely sunk the character of the people in the eyes of the rest of the world; it has covered the face of the country with desolation, and filled the minds of its sorrowing inhabitants with mourning, lamentation, and woe: but above all, it has confirmed them in the darkest and most shameful ignorance, and rivetted them more closely than ever in the bonds of a ridiculous and abominable superstition, to the utter exclusion of a more amiable and rational belief. All these evils, and many others, has slavery accomplished; in return for which the Europeans, for whose benefit, and by whose connivance and encouragement it has flourished so extensively, have given to the heartless natives but ardent and intoxicating spirits, tawdry silk dresses, and paltry necklaces of beads!

The day after the arrival of the Brazen at Badagry (the 29th of November), the gentlemen of the mission, and the officers of the ship, assembled on the quarter-deck to take a final farewell of each other; and some of the latter were deeply affected, as with a faltering voice and agitated manner they breathed their hopes that success might attend the perilous undertaking to which their enterprising friends had so willingly devoted themselves. There was something so moving in the pathetic spectacle of Englishmen parting under a strong persuasion, almost amounting to a conviction, of meeting no more in *this* world; in seeing the manly resolution and stubborn indifference of British officers combating with the tenderer and more amiable feelings of human nature, that I myself could with difficulty stifle my emotion; and to dispel the gloom which hung upon my mind, I bade the officers a hasty and respectful adieu, and shaking hands with many of the honest seamen on deck, I sprang into a canoe that lay alongside the Brazen; and as two of the natives were rowing it towards the shore, I took the opportunity of playing " *Over the hills and far away,*" on a small bugle horn which I had brought with me. This elicited the admiration of the sailors of the ship, and I landed amidst the hearty cheers and acclamations of them all.

Shortly afterwards Captains Clapperton and Pearce, and Dr. Morrison, with Pasko and Dawson,* also landed; but Columbus the mulatto, who had been ill almost from the period of his leaving England, was too weak to accompany them.

* George Dawson, an English seaman, was engaged at Badagry, as servant to Dr. Morrison, and accompanied that gentleman as far as Enguâ, where he died.

The landing was rendered extremely dangerous by reason of a tremendous surf, which rolled violently, and to a great height, for many miles along the coast, and the canoe in which Mr. Houtson (an English merchant, who was taken on board at Whydah, for the purpose of accompanying the mission,) was conveyed from the Brazen, with astronomical instruments, &c. was swamped when at some distance from the beach. This accident had nearly cost that gentleman his life; for after being tossed about on the foam and waves for a few minutes, his strength utterly forsook him, and he ceased to struggle with the waters. In this perilous state he was observed by two of the blacks who had been with him in the ill-fated canoe; and, at the imminent risk of their own lives, the men succeeded in conveying Mr. Houtson, although totally insensible, to the shore, where proper remedies having been administered, he shortly afterwards recovered. The natives subsequently dived after the instruments, &c. and were fortunate enough to regain the whole, although being seriously damaged by the water, many of them were of little, if any, use afterwards.

Neither an English boat, nor a canoe of the ordinary form, can possibly live, even a single minute, in this dreadful surf; and the natives have canoes of singular construction, and exceedingly strong, made purposely to brave its violence; yet, as the preceding casualty clearly shows, even these are insufficient to preserve the passenger from the danger apprehended. The canoes here spoken are of immense size and thickness, and manned by nineteen naked men, who are well skilled in the art of rowing. On every occasion a Fetish-man, covered from head to foot with *gris-gris,* stands in the bow invoking the " Spirit of the Waters" to be propitious, and quell the raging of the sea. He continues alternately watching the motion of the billows and praying in a low mournful tone till the boat reaches the shore or the vessel, when thanks are immediately returned to the water-divinity. When he fancies his petition has been heard, the Fetish-man, catching a favourable opportunity, suddenly claps his hands in a transport, and exclaims, with violent gesticulation and wildness of manner, " i yaw, i yaw ! " (now is the time, now is the time,) which inspires his countrymen in the canoe with fresh energy, and dashing their paddles into the water, they propel their enormous bark through the foamy waves with the swiftness of lightning.

I must own, I was by no means sorry that Columbus did not proceed with us; he was a man of strong and easily excited passions, and was besides malicious and revengeful. He used to take offence at the most trifling accident in the world, and with oaths and bitter imprecations, curse the individual whom he conceived had been the author of it, vowing at the same time to be revenged. He frequently declared, during the voyage, that he himself would be the solitary survivor of the party : all the others, he affirmed, would die before they had been in the country many weeks, and he should have the *pleasure* of returning alone; nevertheless he was himself the very first victim to the effects of that climate which he had proudly boasted could not be prejudicial to him,—for being subsequently landed at Whydah, and overtaking Dr. Dickson at Abomey, he proceeded with that gentleman on the road to Shar, but being attacked with fever, expired, I have been informed, before they had reached that place.

A day or two previously to our leaving the ship, I had by some means or other unintentionally offended Columbus; the next time he saw me, he exclaimed, grinning horribly, in a tone and gesture which could not be mistaken, and which I shall not easily forget, " I shall one day have the pleasure of seeing you parching with thirst on the back of a camel; and rather than give you one drop of water by —— you shall perish there; *that* will be my revenge!"

CHAPTER III.

The Travellers reach Badagry, and leave that city on the 7th of December—Dr. Morrison's illness—Arrival at Latoo—Captain Pearce and the Author attacked with fever—Enter Jannah—Continued and alarming illness of the party—Their progress—Dr. Morrison returns to Jannah.

AT the distance of about half a mile from the beach we came to a small creek, near the mouth of which was a solitary fetish-hut, ornamented in front with a species of small shining stone, which abounds in the country. Near this sacred spot were deposited several bundles of wood, and various articles of earthenware of rude manufacture; but not a single individual could any where be seen. In such reverence are these pagan temples held by the natives, that property, how valuable soever it may be, placed within a certain distance of them, is considered as being under the special protection of their gods; in consequence of which, though it may remain unclaimed for any length of time, it is rarely known to be damaged or stolen.

After crossing the river Formosa, which is about a mile in width, we arrived at Badagry at five o'clock in the afternoon, and were comfortably accommodated in the dwelling of Mr. Houtson who had previously resided at that place. The house, like every other in the town, except the king's, is constructed of bamboo cane, and has but one story. On Friday, the 2d of December, the King, Adólee, sent us a present of a bullock, a fine pig, and some fowls; and on the following day honoured us with a visit, in all the pomp and barbarous magnificence of African royalty. He was mounted on a diminutive black horse, and followed by about one hundred and fifty of his subjects, who danced and capered before and behind him; whilst a number of musicians, performing on native instruments of the rudest description, promoted considerably the animation and vivacity of their motions and gestures. He was gorgeously arrayed in a scarlet cloak, literally covered with gold lace, and white kerseymere trowsers similarly embroidered. His hat was turned up in front with rich bands of gold lace, and decorated with a splendid plume of white ostrich feathers, which, waving gracefully over his head, added not a little to the imposing dignity of his appearance! Close to the horse's head marched two boys, each carrying a musket in his right hand; they wore plain scarlet coats, with white collars and large cocked hats, tastefully trimmed with gold lace, which costly material all classes excessively admire. Two fighting chiefs accompanied their sovereign on foot, and familiarly chatted with him as he advanced. On approaching within a short distance of us, the monarch dismounted, and squatting himself on the ground outside our house, an umbrella was unfurled and held over his head, whilst a dozen of his wives stood round their lord and master

" With diverse-colour'd fans, whose wind did seem
To glow the *delicate* cheeks which they did cool!"

for the atmosphere was sultry and the heat oppressive. After paying our respects to our august visitor,—to do him honour, I was desired to hoist an English union-jack over him. This was the climax of his glory and his pride; he was sensibly delighted, and looked as childishly vain as a girl when she first puts on a new dress. All hands now began to drink rum, and the spectacle became highly and singularly grotesque. Laying aside all pretensions to superiority of rank, his Badagrian majesty forgot his illustrious birth, and was as cheerful and merry as the meanest and most jovial of his subjects. Seated on the ground, his splendid dress glittering in the rays of the sun, surrounded by his generals, pages, and wives, with a British flag held by a white floating over his princely head,—his soul softened by the most inspiring and delicious music! and his animal spirits exhilarated by large and repeated draughts of his favourite cordial,—he was in a transport of joy, and looked and spoke as if he had been the happiest man in the universe; while the shouts and bustle of the people, the cracking of fingers and clapping of hands, the singing, and dancing, and capering, all was so novel, and so African, that it made an impression on my memory which will never be erased from it. This debauch continued for a couple of hours; when all the rum being consumed, and Adólee becoming rather tipsy, his majesty begged me to favour him, before his departure, with a tune on my bugle horn, of which he had formed the most extravagant notions. To this modest request I cheerfully acceded, and played several English and Scotch airs, until I became so completely exhausted that my breath was entirely spent, the king not permitting me to drop the instrument till then. Owing either to the effects of the liquor Adólee had partaken of so freely, or to the sound of the music, &c. he was quite in an extasy, and shook hands and thanked me at the close of every tune. The king then remounted, and the procession returned in the same order, and performed the same anticks as when it came. Captain Clapperton and his associates accompanied the monarch to his palace; whilst I and my companions repaired to our peaceful habitation.

Adólee, recovered from the fatigue and revelry of the preceding day, visited us again on the third, and minutely examined every article belonging to the mission, without, however, expressing the slightest inclination to reserve any thing for himself. When the use of the telescope was explained to him, he could not conceal his astonishment, and fancied its maker to be more than mortal; the medicine-chest also, and its contents, excited his curiosity and attention, and he quitted us with an exalted opinion of the knowledge and ingenuity of the English people.

His majesty, without pomp or ceremony, visited us daily till the period of our departure from his capital; he had the reputation of being a friendly, good sort of man, and was apparently about forty or forty-five years of age, five feet nine inches in height, and rather inclining to corpulency.

The market, which is held daily, is tolerably supplied with poultry, yams, maize, palm wine, country cloth, &c. &c. The cattle are no better, either in size or condition, than those at Sierra Leone, and on other parts of the coast.

On Wednesday, the 7th, after a drinking

EXPOSED NIGHT-QUARTERS. 51

revel with the Badagrian great men, we embarked in canoes on a branch of the Lagos river, accompanied by Adólee and many of his chiefs, in separate canoes, and people in armed boats for our mutual protection, in case of surprise or attack. Landing about a mile and a half from the junction of the Gazie creek, Adólee and some of his people returned to Badagry, and we slept in the evening on the western bank, in the open air, without even the shelter of a single tree. The moon shone brightly and beautifully in the night, and not a sound disturbed the solemn tranquillity of the place, all being as still and quiet as the grave. Next morning we found ourselves wet to the skin with the heavy dew that had fallen in our sleep; and in all probability were thus sown the seeds of those disorders which subsequently broke out with such fatal virulence, and produced suffering, disease, and death, in our little party. In the forenoon I accompanied my master and Mr. Houtson to Bookhar, a neighbouring town, and the stores and baggage were ordered to be sent after us. On arriving at that place we seated ourselves under the branches of a large tree, and were quickly visited by hundreds of the inhabitants, who came in large companies to view us, and as soon as their curiosity was satisfied, made way for their impatient countrymen. The children, who were not tall enough to catch a glimpse of us through the crowd, were perched on the shoulders of their parents or relatives, who pointed us out to them, observing, " There they are !" as if we had been wild beasts, or monsters of some sort. All, however, behaved with the strictest propriety, and although they repeatedly laughed to each other on making observations on the singularity of our appearance or the whiteness of our skin, not a single word of derision or disrespect was uttered against the strangers.

Whilst we were stared at in this manner, the crowd suddenly divided in order to make way for a fighting chief belonging to the army of the king of Katunga, who came in full state to visit us, riding on a small horse, and followed by a large retinue, two of whom were also mounted. On his head he wore a cap and feathers, evidently of European manufacture, and he was clad in a scarlet jacket, fluttering in rags, with dirty yellow facings, and loose trousers of faded nankeen—a dress of which he was extravagantly vain. The king's messengers having had a consultation with the chief, the latter dismounted, and sat himself down at the distance of about a stone's-throw from our tree. Captain Clapperton then sent him an umbrella as a token that we were amicably disposed towards him, and wished him well; on receipt of which his attendants set up so terrific a noise, with drums, clapping of hands, &c. that it was utterly impossible to hear ourselves speak while it lasted. As soon as this clamour had subsided the chief arose, and coming up to us, shook hands with each, very complacently seating himself by our sides. He expressed himself overjoyed at seeing white men, and complimented the English, in no measured language, for the good they had done in trading with the people of the country. A glass or two of rum, which he swallowed with peculiar delight, set the warrior-chief in better humour than ever, and he repeated his encomiums in so loud a key that they were heard by his attendants, who, out of respect, had retreated several yards from the spot, when the music of the drum was revived with greater spirit than before, interrupted only by immense clapping of hands, and other demonstrations of joy. This " harmony of sweet sounds" continued till the mighty chief left us, which took place the moment he perceived that no more spirits were forthcoming.

As soon as we had fairly got rid of our garrulous visitor, we rose to pay a visit to the caboceer, or chief of the town, whom we found in earnest conversation with his elders, and a few of his old grey-headed wives, altogether forming the most venerable looking group of human beings I ever saw. The profoundest silence prevailed as we drew near, and every eye was anxiously fixed upon us. The chief was a tall thin man, well stricken in years, and respectably dressed in a silk tobe and trousers of country cloth. On his head he wore a cap so thickly studded with various coloured glass beads that the material of which it was composed could with difficulty be distinguished; and small gold colored tassels of beads hung from it to the shoulders. The cap was neatly and fancifully made, and set off the black ill-natured face of its owner to great advantage. After paying the usual compliments, goora nuts and water were presented, and my master explaining to the chief who and what we were, and what motives had induced us to visit the country, with which he expressed himself perfectly well satisfied, we were conducted to his residence; receiving shortly afterwards a present of a sheep, some yams, and fire-wood. Many of the chief's young wives stole every opportunity to peep through holes in the walls at the white men, but when detected gratifying their curiosity in this manner, they were excessively confused, and ran off and hid themselves.

In the evening Captain Pearce arrived with the baggage from the banks of the river; and in the night it was guarded by the soldiers of the king of Badagry, who serenaded us till the next morning with a most astounding concert of drums, &c. in order, as they asserted, to deter thieves from plundering the goods.

Near the entrance of the town, on the left side of the road, stands a solitary fetish-hut, of large dimensions, with a number of wooden figures, carved in bas-relief, some in a kneeling and some in a recumbent posture, placed outside the walls; these idols the inhabitants worship, and ascribe miraculous powers to their agency.

We arose at an early hour on Thursday: but the old hypocritical chief, alleging that he had not received a present proportionate to his respectability or expectations, would neither exert himself in any way to procure a single individual to convey the baggage, nor appeared willing for us to leave till he had finished a long-winded harangue, which had already occupied three hours, and threatened to last at least as many more, when his tongue was fortunately stopped by the two Badagrian Generals clapping their hands on his lips. Owing to this circumstance a few individuals only volunteered to assist us, amongst whom was one of the chief's daughters, a bouncing woman of five-and-twenty, who carried the canteen,—so that our Badagrian escort were obliged to undertake that office themselves. We were equally unfortunate in our inquiries for hammock-men, not a single individual in the town being willing to engage himself in what all ranks conceive to be an occupation fit only for horses; but Captain Clapperton having borrowed the horse of a Badagrian chief, he and Mr. Houtson agreed to ride him in turns. We took a short route across the country, whilst Captain Pearce and Dr. Morrison proceeded to Dagnoo by a safer but more circuitous road.

It was evening when we left Bookhar, and it soon becoming dark, we had to grope our way on a narrow foot path, winding through a gloomy dismal forest, and rendered almost impervious to man or beast, except on the beaten track, by reason of thick entangling underwood. To add to our misery, Captain Clapperton became so painfully galled in consequence of riding on the back of a lean horse without a saddle, that he preferred walking the remainder of the way, although wearing only slippers; these were soon lost, and he was obliged to limp a considerable distance barefooted, so that his feet were swollen, and blistered dreadfully, and before reaching Isako were literally bathed in blood.

We were informed in the village that the party with the baggage had left that place some time before for Dagnoo, whither we were obliged to follow it, preceded by a number of the kind inhabitants with burning torches to show us the intricate path, which did not, however, prevent our stumbling at every step. We arrived at Dagnoo about midnight, our clothes being torn to ribbons, and all of us excessively fatigued from the effects of so long and unpleasant a walk; and on finding that the beds had been sent still further on, we were again under the necessity of sleeping in the open air, exposed to a heavy dew, which completely saturated the remnant of our dress before morning.

We arose early, and after crossing a small creek in the vicinity of Dagnoo, continued our journey, through a vast primeval forest, sometimes broken by a grove of palm-trees, a field of Indian corn, and even a whole village in large open places. We were met in the path by numbers of the natives of both sexes, with bundles of palm-leaves on their heads, used for the purpose of thatching their huts; and the wild shrill cry of the grey parrot resounded from the huge branches of the trees.

On arriving at Humba, we found Captain Pearce and Dr. Morrison at the chief's residence, waiting to receive us; and shortly afterwards Captain Clapperton was taken very unwell with fever, having had a slight attack of ague in the course of the day. The town was in ruins, and its inhabitants appeared in a truly pitiable state; nevertheless singing and dancing, and music-playing, were kept up during the whole of the night, with as much spirit and good humour as if the people had been the happiest in the world.

On the morning of the 11th the baggage was sent on, and we walked to another village at no great distance from Humba, although my master was so extremely weak that he was barely able to undertake even so short a journey on foot. When we entered the place, we found the carriers detained by command of the chief, until a flask of rum, by way of tribute, was given him. He came up as soon as he saw us, with a leopard's skin thrown carelessly over his shoulders, and repeated his determination not to let the men proceed till his request was complied with. The old man was however satisfied with a strong glass of grog, prepared for him by Mr. Houtson, each mouthful of which, instead of swallowing, he adroitly squirted into the mouths of his longing attendants, who stood gaping, with glistering eyes, to receive the liquor thus deliciously refined, and which was relished by the whole party with peculiar satisfaction! The carriers were then allowed to go on with the baggage without further molestation, and Captain Clapperton got into a hammock; but the bearers had proceeded only a few paces, when it was for some unaccountable reason suddenly let down, and the fellows scampered away as fast as their legs could carry them. It was afterwards taken up by our own party, and conveyed through Ackongujie, a pleasant village surrounded by fertile land, to a town called Eto, in which the bearers were changed, and we proceeded through thick woods till we arrived at Sattoo, where we slept, after having made an excellent supper on a goat the chief had sent us. Next morning we pursued our journey early, and at noon reached the pleasant town of Bidgie, near to which were extensive plantations of corn and plantains. The chief, a fine young man named Lollakelli, who was perpetually smiling, pressed us to stay with him the remainder of the day; and the inhabitants, who came in crowds to see us, passing the same compliment, after a little hesitation it was accepted, and we slept there.

Dr. Morrison felt himself indisposed in the evening, with slight symptoms of fever, and swelling of the legs; but next morning being partially recovered, we proceeded in good spirits to the borders of a river we had to cross, Lollakelli, with several of his people accompanying us. Mr. Houtson and myself embarked in the first canoe, but we were an hour and half on the water before we could reach the landing-place, situated on the eastern bank: nor did the other canoes meet with better success. All being at length safely over, we pursued our journey, and our road lying nearly the whole of the way through a dried swamp overgrown with rushes, travelling was thereby rendered extremely uncomfortable. About mid-day my master became exhausted, in consequence of fatigue and the excessive heat; and resting himself in the shade of some diminutive trees for a few minutes, a person on horseback passed by, who seeing him reposing on the earth, dismounted, and offered him the use of his horse. This being gratefully accepted, the party was immediately in motion, and the generous black walked with us to Atalabora. On entering that village we found the baggage detained for want of carriers, who had been sent for from an adjoining town, and had not then arrived; so that Captain Pearce, who felt seriously indisposed, and Dr. Morrison, the other invalid, thought it necessary to refresh themselves with an hour or two's sleep, in the principal hut in the town; whilst Mr. Houtson, my master, and myself, took the opportunity of stretching ourselves at full length underneath the branches of a spreading tree, the heat being oppressive, and unrelieved by a single zephyr. The expected carriers having arrived, and the sick expressing themselves somewhat strengthened with the short nap they had enjoyed, they were first sent forwards, and the other gentlemen, with myself, followed them. The road was quite level, and lay through a small town called Funnie, across rich plantations of yams. Towards evening we were met by a person from the chief of Laboo, with horses for our accommodation. We immediately mounted the beasts, and journeying at an easy rate, entered Laboo by moonlight.

The town is delightfully situated on a rising ground, commanding an extensive and noble prospect; the approach to it is through a beautiful walk of trees, between which at certain measured distances, fetish-houses are erected, which are held in the greatest veneration by the inhabitants. Immediately on our arrival we were conducted to the chief, whom we found sitting under the verandah of his dwelling, and who politely welcomed us to Laboo, observing that he had been anxiously expecting us for some hours before. Goora nuts, as usual, were presented, with water in a certain chamber utensil which shall be nameless, the odd service to which it was applied causing us to laugh heartily; and the chief became as sociable after we had been in his company a few minutes only, as if he had been acquainted with us for years. Dr. Morrison was brought into the town about two hours after, in a weak and helpless state; and on Wednesday the 14th, I was myself taken extremely unwell with *coup-de-soleil*, or sun-stroke, having incautiously left my head uncovered for some time on the preceding day. Captain Pearce also felt much worse towards the evening of the 14th, so that the day after that gentleman, and Dr. Morrison and myself, were obliged to be conveyed in hammocks on men's heads, to Jannah, where we arrived an hour before the rest of the party.

The inhabitants quickly surrounded the tree

under which we had been placed, and teazed us with a thousand questions which we were unable to answer. Meantime a dense crowd had collected in front of us, and welcomed the *red* men as we were termed, (our skin being at that time much blistered by the rays of the sun,) by drumming, and singing and dancing. In our languid state, we were ill able to bear this eternal din, and entreated the people to conduct us to a hut, for that we were very ill; but they answered with the greatest unconcern, that the king, whose house was directly opposite, must of necessity see us before we ventured to stir from the spot; that he was the greatest man between Badagry and Katunga; and that it would not be well for us to offend him by being too importunate in our solicitations. We at length lost all patience, and observing a large empty shed in the centre of the square, which we found to be the palàver-house or hall of council, we ventured to crawl into it as well as we could, being only a few yards from the tree. Captain Pearce and Dr. Morrison had then their beds made; but mine being rolled up, I was too weak to spread it, and so I lay along the bare ground. As soon as Captain Clapperton and Mr. Houtson had made their appearance, the noise was hushed for a moment, and shortly afterwards the chief himself, accompanied by about fifty of his wives, approached, and, whilst they stationed themselves at a short distance from us, the latter struck up a native tune, which they sang loudly, and with much feeling; indeed there was a solemnity and pathos about it that reminded me of the most impressive church-music of my own country. As soon as the sound of the ladies' voices had ceased, the band played a lively air, in which the singers occasionally joined; and at the conclusion of the concert a message was sent from the king to the palàver-house, for the *red men* that were well to make their appearance. Accordingly Captain Clapperton and Mr. Houtson went to the chief, who, at the opening of the conference, I could perceive, as I lay on the earth, to be violently agitated speaking with great apparent anger, and pointing several times to a silver knife that was stuck in his girdle. After knitting his brows, and frowning for a minute or two, his features suddenly relaxed into a gentler expression, and graciously smiling, he shook hands cordially with the gentlemen, and entering the palàver-house, extended his royal hand to us for the like purpose. He was attired in a loose yellow silk tobe, and trousers of country cloth; and his cap of red velvet had a purple silk tassel appended to the crown. Like most of his countrymen, the chief or king of Jannah was fond of displaying his conversational powers, and when answering any questions that were put to him, or making observations on what struck him as being singular or remarkable in our appearance, he rattled a child's silver whistle and bells (of English manufacture), which he held in his left hand, by way of accompaniment to his voice, which was certainly not the most harmonious in the world.

We were subsequently conducted to a house which was partly occupied, and too small for our accommodation; so that my master, Mr. Houtson, and Dawson were obliged to remain under the verandah, neither of the others being well enough to follow their example. In the evening the king came alone, and plainly dressed, to visit us, and in this instance was very inquisitive and communicative. He wished particularly to understand our business with the sultan of Yariba, for, as we afterwards learnt, a messenger from the coast had informed him that the white men's object was expressly and solely to make war upon that monarch and dethrone him; but the sorry plight in which we then were disproved the assertion; and the chief himself acknowledged that he did not place the slightest confidence in the unfounded rumour.

On Friday I became considerably worse, and on the following day my life was despaired of. In the evening I was bled in the temple; but the doctor, who was himself suffering from fever, being unable to hold the instrument steadily, inadvertently thrust it into my skull. This accident occasioned the most excruciating agony, and made me shriek with pain. I passed the night in a manner that cannot be described, but next morning felt much easier and better. On Monday, however, the fever returned with more violence than ever, attended by a severe head-ache that almost drove me distracted, and at my own suggestion Dr. Morrison ordered my head to be shaved. To perform this delicate operation a native barber was at length found, who came wielding a tremendous knife curved like a reap-hook, instead of a razor, and began his avocation in a most brutal manner, just like a clumsy English butcher shaving a slaughtered pig; insomuch, that when his labour was finished, my skull was scalped almost as effectually as if it had been done by the tomahawk of a North American Indian. Although my head was thus miserably excoriated, a large blister, covering the whole of it, was applied; and my suffering was heightened to the utmost degree of intensity; so that I lost my reason, and in the evening was completely delirious. In this state, as I subsequently learnt, I sprang from my couch, and being animated with the fury of a maniac, knocked down the doctor and my master, broke and destroyed every thing within my reach, and when in the act of escaping in my night-dress from the door, was forcibly dragged back to my bed by the united strength of the whole party, who had been alarmed with the noise I had made. Weakened and exhausted by this mad prank, the phrenzy left me, and reason returned, but with it came the loss of speech. About an hour afterwards a consultation was held by my bed-side; and the doctor having carefully felt my pulse, I was comforted by the expressed opinion, that it would be impossible for me to live throughout the night. Much to the astonishment of all, however, on Tuesday the disorder had abated so greatly, that I was enabled to sit up and converse rationally with those around me: my health, in fact, seemed to return almost as rapidly as I had lost it.

Dr. Morrison and Captain Pearce, in the meantime, continued alarmingly ill, and evidently getting worse. Their hollow eyes, sunk deeply in their sockets, and their skin exhibiting a sallow and cadaverous hue, they looked more like walking spectres than living human beings; insomuch, that Captain Clapperton, distressed at their altered appearance, urged upon each of them the necessity of their either remaining at Jannah, or returning, under the care of Mr.

Houtson, to the Brazen. Both gentlemen, however, declared their invincible repugnance to the measure, and on the contrary expressed themselves resolutely bent to proceed at all risks: Captain Pearce, in particular, felt greatly hurt at the suggestion of his friend, and asserted, in a decided tone, that he would infinitely prefer being buried in the country, remote as it was from his native land, than suffer Captain Clapperton to pursue his journey alone, while he had life to accompany him. The Captain, affectionately pressing the hand of the disinterested invalid, thanked him for the lively interest he felt in his welfare, but repeated his unwillingness for either him or Dr. Morrison to proceed further, in their present emaciated and languid state: to this, however, no attention was paid.

Things being thus amicably adjusted, to the complete satisfaction at least of the invalids, we left Jannah early on the morning of Thursday the 22d, (the sick, myself amongst the number, travelling in hammocks, as on former occasions,) and slept at Beechy that night. At ten the next morning we arrived at Tschow, in which town we received much hospitality from the natives; and in the afternoon Dr. Morrison, fancying that the sea air would restore his health, which was hourly declining, at his own suggestion was sent back to the ship, under the protection of Mr. Houtson.

CHAPTER IV.

Deaths of Dawson, Captain Pearce, and Dr. Morrison—Their funeral—The survivors, after meeting with various occurrences, and experiencing the kindest hospitality from the natives on their route, arrive at Katunga, the capital of Yariba, on the 15th of January, 1826.

On Saturday, the roads being rendered almost impassable, in consequence of the rains that had fallen the preceding night, it was not without experiencing considerable difficulty that we could pursue our journey. The mud and water reached, in some places, almost to the horses' shoulders; and Dawson, who was ill with ague, was unable to retain his seat on the animal's back, and fell three or four times in the mire, till he became so much exhausted by struggling to regain his seat, that, in despair, he at last flung his arms only across the horse's back; and panting with his exertions, was in this manner dragged to a considerable distance. At eleven o'clock we arrived at the village of Egbo; and after partaking of a slight refreshment, each of us being indisposed in a greater or less degree, we stretched ourselves at full length on our mats, in the hope of obtaining a little sleep. Dawson, however, was taken dreadfully ill, and his moanings of distress prevented me from closing my eyes. He pronounced the names of his wife and children, whom he had left in England, with a bitter emphasis, and reproached himself repeatedly with having deserted them, to perish miserably in a strange country. In this manner he complained till the afternoon, refusing all consolation, when he became a little more composed; and Captain Pearce fell asleep. My master had quitted the apartment just before; and the medicine-chest lying open by Dawson's side, he perceived it, and pointing to a phial, desired a black attendant to fill him a glass of its contents; which being promptly done, he eagerly swallowed it. Whilst this was going on I had fallen into a slumber; and on awaking, about a quarter of an hour afterwards, not hearing Dawson's groans, I asked how he did; but receiving no answer, I went to his bed-side, and found him a cold and stiffened corpse! The sight of so unexpected and ghastly a spectacle caused me to shudder, and I involuntarily made an exclamation of surprise and terror, that awoke Captain Pearce, who asked what was the matter. Before I had time to reply, he had raised himself on his couch, and the truth instantly bursting upon him — "What!" said he, " is Dawson dead? Well, poor fellow, *his* sufferings are over; *I* cannot long survive him;" and with a deep sigh he sunk back exhausted on his mat, without making any further remark.

On examining the bottle from which the unfortunate man had desired the liquor to be taken, I found it to be partly filled with *ether*, which he must have mistaken for something else, and which had caused his almost immediate dissolution. As soon as the natives were made acquainted with the circumstance, they set up their death-yell; and if all the fiends of darkness had joined in chorus, they could not have produced an effect more frightfully and fearfully appalling than was the sound produced in that instance. Captain Clapperton hastened to silence them, which, after some difficulty, he succeeded in doing; but the awfully terrific noise the people made, seemed to be ringing in our ears the whole of the night. As dead bodies cannot be left exposed a great while in tropical countries, Dawson was buried on the evening of his death, followed to the grave by the whole of our black attendants and myself. Captain Clapperton read the funeral service over his remains, which were then deposited in the earth, and we returned to Captain Pearce, whom we had left alone in the hut. Our party was now reduced to three whites, one of whom was dangerously ill; my master himself was in a much worse state of health than he would either acknowledge or believe; and I was but just recovering from a disease that had nearly proved fatal to me. A gloom was therefore cast upon the countenances of our little band, as we prepared to proceed, on the morning of Sunday; but Captain Pearce rallying a little, we set off in more cheerful spirits.

The appearance of the country, from Jannah to Tshow, is greatly superior to that from the coast to the former place, being clearer of wood, and in a higher state of cultivation, swelling likewise into easy and delightful undulations. Streams of water fertilize the vallies; and the hills, covered with a lively verdure, are adorned with lofty and handsome trees. The towns of the natives, from Badagry to Tshow, with a few exceptions only, like those in the island of Madagascar, are situated in the bosom of thick woods, and are entered by paths so intricate, that, like the labyrinth of Woodstock, they are known to none but the inhabitants themselves. Sometimes, however, they have only one path, which is generally defended by strong stockades or a mud wall, and sometimes by both together.

On Tuesday morning we continued our journey, with a cool strengthening breeze and a serene atmosphere, which seemed to invigorate each of us with renewed life and spirit; and, after two hours' travelling, we arrived at Engwà. In the course of the journey, for the first time since leaving the ship, we perceived great numbers of trees, stripped of their foliage, and the grass beaten to the ground, so that, with the exception of the absence of frost and snow, the country looked like many parts of England in the month of November or December. Several of the natives in this, as in almost every other instance, either accompanied or followed us on the way, and we experienced as much civility from them as our countrymen would have bestowed upon us in our native land. They were, generally speaking, neatly dressed in cap, shirt (tobe), and trousers, and very cleanly in their personal appearance.

About eleven o'clock Captain Pearce became suddenly worse, and an hour or two afterwards was delirious. He talked much and incoherently, in detached sentences; at one time apparently conversing with his mother in the most affectionate terms, asking her questions, and answering them himself, and the next moment reverting to his own melancholy condition, and muttering something which no one could understand. In this pitiable state he remained till nine o'clock in the evening, when he fell into a stupor, from which he awoke about half an hour afterwards, and attempting to raise himself on his couch, with a faint groan, and a convulsive throe, he fell back and instantly expired.

Both Captain Clapperton and myself were deeply affected as we enveloped the lifeless body in its shroud; and a host of gloomy reflections crowded upon our minds, to see the once spirited and cheerful companion of our wanderings stretched out before us, the shadow only of a man, clothed in the mournful habiliments of death. Next morning, about eleven o'clock, the body was borne to the place of its interment, followed by my master and myself, with the messengers of the kings of Badagry and Katunga, and a great number of natives, who all behaved with the strictest decorum. As in the former instance, Captain Clapperton, although extremely unwell, in a tremulous voice and agitated manner, read the funeral service, interrupted only by his own emotion, which he found it impossible to conceal. The corpse having been consigned to the grave, it was soon closed over him for ever, and my master and myself, with heavy hearts and melancholy anticipations, returned to our cheerless habitation. The following inscription, at the desire of Captain Clapperton, I carved on a board, which was placed at the head of the pit, over which a shed was built by the natives; and a strong bamboo fence surrounded the whole : —

" Here lie the remains of Robert Pearce, Captain in the Royal Navy of England, who died 27th Dec. 1825, aged 28, much regretted by those that survive of the mission.

"H. CLAPPERTON.
"R. LANDER."

Captain Pearce had rendered himself a general favourite by his gentle and pleasing manners, and excellent natural disposition. My master was particularly attached to him, and esteemed him highly, while the natives almost adored him. His companionable qualities were great, and he displayed them to advantage in our toilsome journeyings, raising the spirits of

TRIBUTE TO CAPTAIN PEARCE. 81

the party by his wit and cheerfulness, and infusing his own good temper into the breasts of every one. He was besides an excellent limner and draughtsman, and possessed an aptitude for picking up the various languages of the natives, which bade fair to render him of the most essential service to the mission. No one deplored his loss, or felt the want of his pleasant society, more than myself. Just after he was taken ill, at his own request, as soon as the day's toil was over, I was constantly with him, and at night my mat was placed close to his. We used to chat for whole hours together, on different circumstances of our lives; and my little history afforded him a fund of amusement. Any thing, indeed, that promised to divert our thoughts from the calamities which threatened us, was resorted to, and every trifling incident we had each met with from our childhood repeated a thousand times over, in order to dole away the long, still, dismal hours of night, when sickness prevented either of us from closing our eyes. Throughout Captain Pearce's illness, his patience, resignation, and manly fortitude never forsook him; he was conscious that he should ultimately sink under the influence of a disorder that was visibly wasting him, and daily reducing his strength: nevertheless, this belief neither shook his firmness nor damped his spirits, and he always spoke of his anticipated dissolution with a serious calmness of manner that surprised and pleased me. None of us thought that his end was so near; we expected he would have struggled on at least a week or two longer; but the sorrowful event disappointed the hopes we had cherished, and he expired prematurely, to the infinite regret of every one.

Mr. Houtson returned on Saturday the 31st, with the afflictive intelligence of the decease of Dr. Morrison, which mournful circumstance occurred at Jannah, by a coincidence, singular in misfortune, on the same day, and as nearly as possible at the same hour as that in which Captain Pearce had breathed his last. He was decently interred by Mr. Houtson on the 28th, near to the house in which they had resided; and the ceremonies of the Church of England were performed over his remains by the same gentleman.

HOSTILE TRIBES. 83

We saw several busts of men, as well as figures of tigers, crocodiles, serpents, &c. carved on blocks of wood, and extremely well executed, at Engwâ. The natives of that part of Africa appear to have a genius for the art of sculpture, which is in great repute with them; and some of their productions rival, in point of delicacy, any of a similar kind that I have seen in Europe.

A fine Portuguese brig, and a Spanish schooner, had been lying near Badagry, on our leaving that place, waiting for slaves; to supply which vessels, the King of Jannah had sent a slaving party to the territories of the Essàs, a powerful tribe in the neighbourhood of Engwâ, which had captured numbers of the people. The Chief of the Essàs was greatly exasperated at this conduct of his neighbour, and had made numerous reprisals; so that, at the period of our passing through the country, a general war was the consequence.

Owing to this circumstance, on leaving the town of Engwâ on the morning of the 3d of January, 1826, we were accompanied by upwards of a hundred men and women, who placed themselves under our protection, fancying that, when within sight of the white strangers, no evil could befall them. We crossed a river called Akkeni at ten o'clock A.M., which was full of sunken rocks, and arrived at the village of Afoora about three hours after. Our journey on that day was rendered particularly pleasant by the fragrant odour exhaled from the cotton plant, then in full blossom—the wild, solitary whistle of the grey parrot, and the delightful melody of hundreds of small birds, swelling from the branches of the tall trees. The country every where improved as we advanced:—fields of Indian corn, and plantations of cotton, were numerous, while groves of palm, and clumps of cocoa and female cocoa trees, scattered on all sides, rendered the prospect from the hills inexpressibly beautiful. Quitting Afoora early on Wednesday, we reached Assula the same morning, in which town we were more conveniently lodged than we had been since leaving the coast.

Starting about seven o'clock the next day, and travelling over several low hills, and through pleasant vallies, we entered Assoudo, (the first walled town we had yet seen,) at noon. In the paths we observed numbers of fine birds, with silky and brilliant plumage, but I could not be informed to what particular species they belonged, neither of us having seen any of a similar kind before. Assoudo contains upwards of ten thousand inhabitants, who were all as curious as their countrymen, and also as noisy, but infinitely more modest and respectful, and consequently more pleasing in their manners. We received an abundant supply of provisions from the chief, consisting of a goat, fowls, eggs, yams, bananas, &c.

On Friday, after halting at Tedi, a small village romantically situated on a beautifully wooded slope, where we changed carriers, we arrived at the town of Choko; but its chief, with nearly the whole of the male inhabitants, being engaged in hunting the buffalo, did not return till evening. In the mean time we had spent an hour or two under a tree, but finding no one disposed to invite us to a house, of our own accord we took peaceable possession of the best hut the place afforded, of the goodness of which, however, we could not boast, it being sadly out of repair.

Our road from Choko, on Saturday, lay round the sides of low mountains, on the summits and in the hollows of which were several hamlets, inhabited by an industrious race, who had extensive plantations in the valleys below, where the palm tree flourishes in great beauty. We slept at Yundekka that night, and on the next day arrived at Duffo. There the inhabitants visited us by thousands, and when desired to go away, they replied that if we did not allow them to visit our house, we must come out, and show ourselves to them in the street, for that they were determined, let the consequence be what it might, to see a white man before they died. The town contains ten or twelve thousand inhabitants, nearly half of whom, on our departure the next morning, followed us at some distance, in order to catch a last glimpse of their white visitants.

We passed through three villages, on the route to Chiadoo, to which we were advancing, viz. Jesin, Weza, and Lukewâ, the chief of each of which, with the people, detained us an hour or more underneath the branches of trees, gazing on us with a mingled sensation of compassion and wonder, till, their curiosity being fully satisfied, we were suffered to proceed. At the latter of these villages elephants' teeth were offered us for sale; but on our refusing to purchase them, on the ground that we were not come for the purpose of trading, the greatest amazement was depicted on the countenances of the people, and they wondered amongst each other what motive besides could possibly attract us to their country.

We entered Chiadoo about six o'clock in the evening, and received the accustomed present of provisions, &c. with the addition of a turkey. The town, seated on a gentle declivity, is densely inhabited, and defended by a thick mud wall and deep trench, which wholly surround it. Within the wall, and almost close to it, trees of large dimensions are planted, so as to form a belt from two to three miles in circumference, which in case of necessity might easily be converted into an excellent means of defence for the inhabitants.

The scenery on the road from Afoora to Chiadoo is extremely picturesque, but the path itself is in many places rugged and dangerous to travellers. Winding by the sides of the *Kong* mountains, over rocks and precipices, or through romantic glens at their base, intersected with innumerable streams, the track was generally covered with small loose stones, which galled the feet of the hammock-men in a pitiable manner. On all sides immense masses of granite, jutting abruptly from the hills or vallies, reared their heads to the height, in some places, of several hundred feet; whilst others, fearfully overhanging the narrow foot-way, caused a shuddering awe to creep over us as we passed underneath them, which could not be suppressed. With some danger, and more difficulty, the men who bore my hammock clambered with me to the summit of one of the mounts, from whence the prospect on the one hand was immeasurably grand and imposing, and on the other enchantingly beautiful. At our feet were lovely dales, cultivated in the highest degree, and planted with cotton, yams, the plantain, &c. fertilized by meandering rivulets, sparkling in the sunbeams; whilst before and behind us were naked rocks, precipitously steep and rugged, many standing singly, and others piled loosely upon each other, apparently ready to tumble to the earth below. The vallies, as well as the slopes and summits of the hills, being studded with the cleanly habitations of the natives, all bore an air of novelty, cheerfulness, beauty, and grandeur, that I have never seen surpassed.

Our carriers having made themselves merry at the village of Weza, with an intoxicating beverage called *otée* (a kind of ale made from millet), were rather frolicsome during the remainder of the journey; and on descending an almost perpendicular precipice, I was in momentary expectation of being tossed head-long from their shoulders, my continued weakness rendering me unfit to walk; but happily my fears were not realized, and after numberless hair-breadth escapes, I was conveyed in safety to Chiadoo. The chief of that town, whose kindness to us was displayed in a striking manner, entreated us to remain with him a few days, and Mr. Houtson being indisposed, and Captain Clapperton still more so, the latter thought it advisable to stay a couple of days at least in the place, in order to try whether ease and quiet would produce a beneficial effect on the health of either of them. On the morning of Thursday, the 12th, we left Chiadoo, followed by the chief and an immense crowd of people of both sexes, amongst whom were hundreds of children, the ladies enlivening us with songs at intervals, and the men blowing on horns and beating on gongs and drums, without any regard to time, forming altogether a most barbarous concert of vocal and instrumental music, which continued to our great inconvenience and annoyance till we arrived at Matoné, when they took leave of us and returned. The carriers refreshed themselves with two huge calabashes of *otée* whilst we remained in the town, after which they started with redoubled vigour, and about one o'clock halted at Arrowâ, where we slept.

After some little difficulty, occasioned by the unwillingness of the chief and inhabitants to part with us so soon, we pursued our journey at half-past nine next morning, and resting awhile at Washoo, entered Chaki in the afternoon. The appearance of the country traversed differed but little from that which has already been described as seen on the road to Chiadoo, with the exception of its being, if possible, yet more varied, and wearing an aspect of still deeper and sterner beauty; hill rising above hill, and rock above rock, in proud magnificence. In some places huge blocks of naked granite seemed split as if by the hands of giants, leaving frightful chasms, the bottoms of which could not be distinctly seen; and in others detached fragments, irregularly scattered over the country, looking wildly and negligently grand, inspired the strongest belief that they had been forcibly rent asunder, at a remote era, by some dreadful convulsion of nature.

The air on the mountains is cooler, clearer, and more salubrious than in the plains below, and the inhabitants seemed to enjoy better health, and as we were informed lived to a more advanced age than their countrymen of the vallies. We were every where received on the road with acclamations and songs of welcome; and as soon as our little party was discerned, all labour immediately ceased. The people assembling in groups of from three or four to fifty, approached as near as the rocks would permit them; and doffing their caps, they greeted us as we passed, wishing us a pleasant journey to their sovereign at Katunga.

On the top of the highest hill of the whole ridge is perched the populous town of Cheki, at an immense elevation from the plains, the approach to which is by a winding path, more steep and rugged than any we had before met with, and up which we were obliged positively to climb on our hands and knees. The chief, who may be styled a petty king, having a considerable number of towns, and many thousands of people under his protection and command,— was seated outside of his house, under its verandah, surrounded by about a hundred of his wives, and musicians with drums and fifes. On our approach the latter struck up a native air, the ladies keeping time with their feet, and accompanying the instruments with their voices, which were so loud and shrill that the sound rent the air. To this *voluptuous* music we were obliged to listen for the space of an hour, when it ceased, and we took the opportunity of paying our respects to the chief, and being completely tired, were conducted to a large hut which had been prepared for our reception. No sooner had we been fairly housed, however, than we were visited, first by several of the inhabitants, whose curiosity was irksome and painful to us, and next by the chief in person, who drank tea, and remained with us till a very late hour, asking us innumerable questions about England, and listening with the most mortifying attention, and intolerable patience, to all we chose to tell him. His countenance was open and pleasing, and in many of his observations he displayed a degree of acuteness and penetration that startled us. We were treated by this chief with a kindness, remarkable even amongst his countrymen, and, under his hospitable roof, we almost forgot all our misfortunes.

Arising early on Saturday, the 14th, though pressed to remain by every inducement that could be thought of, we departed from Chaki at eight o'clock, attended by the mountain-chief, with upwards of two hundred of his wives, and a long train of people. Passing for the first time through several Falatah villages, whose inhabitants were chiefly employed in the occupations of pasturage and agriculture, Mr. Houtson and myself entered the walled town of Koofo at one, and about an hour after Captain Clapperton was brought into the town on a hammock, being still severely indisposed. Several extensive cotton plantations lay near the road, and the soil, generally speaking, was clear of wood, and tolerably well cultivated. The town of Koofo has a double wall, and is the largest we had noticed, containing, in all probability, fully twenty thousand inhabitants. We were saluted with the usual demonstrations of African welcome on entering the gates; and in the afternoon of our arrival, and the next day, the spacious court or yard with which we were accommodated was literally crammed with people of both sexes, and of all ages; and their impertinent curiosity it was utterly impossible to satisfy. As soon as one party had stayed as long as they thought proper, another supplied its place, in such rapid succession, that, till the evening of each day had been pretty far advanced, we had not a moment to call our own.

The further we penetrated into the country, the more dense we found the population to be, and civilization became at every step more strikingly apparent. Large towns at the distance of only a few miles from each other, we were informed lay on all sides of us, the inhabitants of which pay the greatest respect to the laws, and live under a regular form of government.

Captain Clapperton, finding himself stronger and better, ventured to leave Koofo on horseback, on Monday at eight o'clock A. M., and after two hours' travelling through a well cultivated and delightful country, studded with pleasant Falatah hamlets, we arrived at Soccasoo. In this town, our messenger having gormandized on a leg of pork, was taken so sick that he either could not or would not proceed, and as we durst not go on without him, we were obliged to abide in the place till the following day.

The opinion that the white men were come as "messengers of peace" was general in the country, and implicitly believed by all ranks. Two years previously to our landing from the Brazen, the Houssa slaves belonging to the Sultan of Yariba had rebelled against their sovereign, and, fleeing into the woods, had built themselves a considerable town, no more than two days' journey from the capital (Katunga), which they called Lori. In it they strongly entrenched themselves, and, by the addition of numbers of their straggling countrymen, who willingly flocked to their standard, had become so formidable in a short time, that they had successfully resisted all the attempts of his Yaribean Majesty to re-enslave them, and maintained their independence against the force of an empire. About the time of our journeying into the interior, it was reported that the insurgents had recently been reinforced by a large body of Falatah horsemen, which proved in fact to be the case, and the news had struck so great a panic into the minds of the people of Yariba, that those residing in the vicinity of the mutinous slaves had emigrated to more remote provinces. Hence the anxious solicitation of every one, that as " messengers of peace," we should compromise matters between their monarch and his refractory vassals, which course could alone inspire the people with the hope of preserving their lives and property. The Houssas had already begun to act on the offensive, and had made frequent incursions, even to the dwellings of their former masters, sacking and setting fire to their towns, and laying their country waste.

On Tuesday the 17th we left Soccasoo, and changing horses at the town of Ladooli, halted at Hadjidibbah, where, both my master and Mr. Houtson becoming sick and ill, we rested for three hours. We then again set forward, the path lying through a forest of stunted trees; and reaching Akkibosa in the afternoon, slept there that night. In the course of the morning we had passed several villages, two or three of which were in ruins, having been partly burnt by the

Houssas, and deserted by their original inhabitants.

The atmosphere was close and sultry on our setting out on the morning of Wednesday, and continued so during the journey. About two hours' travelling brought us to the walled town of Adja, the entrance to which is through a spacious avenue of noble trees. Here we were obliged to stop for the remainder of the day, because the inhabitants were at work in the plantations. At an early hour on Thursday, the chief, who had been informed the previous evening of the complaint under which Captain Clapperton laboured, came with a dose of medicine for him to take; but after swallowing it my master became so dreadfully ill, that Mr. Houtson, as well as myself, suspected that poison had been administered to him. In this conjecture, however, we were happily deceived; for in about two hours the pain, which had been occasioned by the potion together with his former ailment, suddenly left him in an extraordinary manner, after which, he expressed himself in perfect health, and ready to proceed. We arrived at Layboo at one o'clock the same day, having seen on the road five towns, two or three of which were walled, and of no inconsiderable extent.

At six next morning we were again in motion, and halting at the village of Bougboug at seven, and at Leogalla, a Falatah town, at eight o'clock, arrived at Ateepa at twelve at noon. The country traversed was agreeably diversified by hills of gentle and gradual ascent, and fertile vallies, cultivated with yams, corn, bananas, &c. Ateepa, like most towns of any magnitude in the country, is furnished with a strong wall, made of earth, and a belt of trees within it, which, by reason of a thorny creeping shrub clinging round the trunks, like the ivy to the oak, and throwing out vigorous shoots, had become so thickly entangled as to form a secure barrier, which, except by the narrow gateway at the entrance, was impervious to man and beast.

On Saturday we departed from Ateepa, attended by the chief and a long train of the male inhabitants, to defend us from any attack that the Borghoo robbers might feel disposed to make on so insignificant a party as ourselves.

At Nannah, a considerable walled town, we changed carriers; and its chief, copying the example of him of Ateepa, joined our procession also, with a strong party, having the same benevolent object in view, and escorted us to Leobadda, where each of the chiefs drank a glass of grog, and returned with their attendants to their respective towns. Leobadda stands close to some huge masses of pale granite rocks, broken into irregular fragments, and has a wall of prodigious thickness. Its population is from six to seven thousand souls, who all seemed to be contentedly poor, invariably happy. The same generous hospitality which had so eminently characterised their countrymen, was displayed by the inhabitants of Leobadda, even in the midst of poverty and rags, with an alacrity and cheerfulness that redound greatly to their credit, and speak volumes in their praise.

At seven o'clock on Sunday, the chief, with many of his people, assembled in front of our house, and accompanied us for some miles. On the road we met several hundreds of men, women, and children, with heavy loads on their heads, who had been travelling the whole of the preceding night, and who appeared so greatly fatigued, as scarcely to be able to drag their lazy limbs after them. They were carefully watched by overseers (one of whom was appointed to each fifty), who were all armed, either with short swords, or bows and arrows, and made the weary travellers quicken their pace by threats of punishment whenever they observed them loitering on the way. We passed in the course of the journey, several villages which had been burnt and destroyed by Falatahs; the walls were overgrown with weeds, and the trees, which a short time before had afforded a grateful and refreshing shade to the inhabitants, seared by the conflagration, and standing blighted and withering, as solitary memorials of the awful manner in which those once flourishing towns had been converted into waste and desolate places. At noon we descended into a delightful valley, situated in the bosom of a ridge of rocks, which effectually hid it from observation till one approached almost close to it. It was intersected with whimpering streams and purling rills, the elegant palm, and the broad leaved banana, covered with foliage, embellishing the sheltered and beautifully romantic spot. In the centre was a sheet of water, resembling an artificial pond, in which were numbers of young maidens from the neighbouring town of Tschow, some of them reposing at full length on its verdant banks, and some frisking and basking in the sun-beams, whilst others of their companions were sporting with the Naiads of the sacred stream; but all of them visibly delighted with the pleasant recreations which they were enjoying so prettily and innocently. We stood for a season gazing on them with pleasure; but no sooner were our white faces observed by the young ladies, than their amusements instantly ceased, and the sable beauties simultaneously rushing from the water, snatched up their apparel, and with their uncovered associates, concealing their faces with their hands, ran away and hid themselves behind the trunks of trees, looking as coy and bashful as did their mother Eve in the garden of Eden.

Leaving that lovely glen with regret, we arrived at Tschow, a walled town, with a good population, at two o'clock. As soon as we could be accommodated with a house, we began cleaning our guns and pistols, as the roads to Katunga were, we had been repeatedly informed, infested with numerous bands of desperadoes, whose success and boldness had terrified, to an alarming degree, the peaceable and timid inhabitants.

On the evening of our arrival, the expected escort from the Sultan of Yariba entered the town. It consisted of two hundred horsemen, and double that number on foot, commanded by a war-chief, and armed with spears, and bows and arrows; all most grotesquely attired, some flouncing in handsome robes, and some fluttering in rags. From the moment of their arrival to the period of our departure, we had not a moment's quiet. They paraded the town all night, vociferously bellowing the happiness they felt, or pretended to feel, on meeting with the white men—serenaded us with a concert of drums, flutes, and trumpets, with powerful vocal accompaniments, and kept shouting and hallooing till we arose in the morning.

All was hurry and confusion as we prepared to depart, and our escort soon getting themselves in readiness, we bade adieu to the chief of Tschow, and started from the town about six o'clock, accompanied by a great number of merchants and others, who cheerfully embraced the opportunity of putting themselves under our protection. Nothing could be more animated than the appearance of our boisterous conductors, winding their way up a narrow and crooked path; the horsemen with their long spears, clearing the road, and hurrying onwards as fast as their jaded and diminutive beasts could walk with them; and the bowmen on foot, with their instruments slung across their shoulders, and quiver full of arrows, appended to their sides, plodding after them with all imaginable haste. But by far the most amusing, if not the most important part of that strange and singular cavalcade, were the musicians themselves, who found it no easy matter to keep pace with their more lively countrymen, and perform on their instruments at the same time. The drummers, flourishing their sticks with a scornful, consequential air; the trumpeters with their black bloated cheeks shining with fat; and the fifers turning up the whites of their eyes towards heaven, and producing altogether the most discordant, most terrific sounds that can be conceived, were highly ludicrous; nor could we, in spite of ourselves, maintain a becoming gravity, or help being infinitely diverted every time that we ventured to look back, and steal a glance at our never-enough-to-be-admired lovers of harmony!

We halted near a village called Achoran at nine o'clock, but the baggage being at some distance behind, we left it to the care of the chiefs, and proceeded with a hundred of the escort, (the road in many places rugged and overshadowed with the branches of trees,) and crossed a stream flowing to the Quorra about an hour after.

At eleven at noon, on attaining the summit of a lofty ridge, we came in sight of the city of Katunga, lying to the south of us, at the base of a granite mountain, and apparently embosomed in beautiful trees. Between the ridge and the city was a fertile valley, highly cultivated, and extending to the westward as far as the eye could reach; while the view to the eastward was bounded by a gigantic rock, shivered into fragments, and at no great distance from the place on which we stood. An hour's easy riding brought us to the north gate of the metropolis of Yariba, outside of which were a fetish-hut, and a few private habitations; and on entering it we took up our abode for the time, at the residence of one of the chiefs of the escort.

As soon as the remainder of the convoy with the baggage had arrived, the intelligence was immediately transmitted to Mansolah, the King, from whom we presently received a warm invitation. After a ride of full five miles through the streets of Katunga, in which we were attended by the escort and musicians, who created so thick a cloud of dust that it had well nigh suffocated us, we at length reached the king's palace. His majesty was seated under the verandah, with two umbrellas spread over him, and surrounded by above four hundred of his wives, with many of his caboceers and other great men. Dismounting at the distance of twenty yards, we walked up almost close to the umbrellas, when Mansolah arose, and very cordially shook hands with each of us, welcoming us to his kingdom with a broad grin, lifting up our hands three several times, and each time exclaiming " Ako! ako!" which means literally " How do you do?" The multitude, the chiefs, and the king's ladies, seemed equally pleased with their good-humoured sovereign at our visit, and displayed the warmth of their feelings by acclamations, shaking of hands, and smiles and encouraging glances. Before our dismissal his majesty enquired more particularly after our respective healths, but made few other observations. In the evening he visited us at our house, attended by his eunuchs and women, and, simply asking how we did, left us with the hope of seeing us again the next day.

CHAPTER V.

Residence at Katunga—Ebo the eunuch—Pantomimic representation by the Yaribeans—Departure from the city of Katunga—Arrival at Khiama—Wow Wow—Manners of the people—Boussa—Mungo Park.

WE remained at Katunga exactly seven weeks; the king, on various frivolous pretexts, refusing to grant us permission to depart before. During all this time each of us enjoyed but indifferent health, Captain Clapperton in particular being oftentimes so severely indisposed as to be unable either to walk or ride; nevertheless we were treated with the utmost civility and kindness by the people generally. The king himself visited us almost every day, and never came without an acceptable present of provisions; while his caboceers behaved with a still nobler generosity, insomuch that if it had not been for the malpractices of a sly, lubberly, fat, monstrous eunuch, named Ebo, to whose care was entrusted our provisions, and whose ravenous appetite was proverbial in the city, we should have been literally crammed with every delicacy both of the country and season. That old gormand had a paunch of a most awful size, which he contrived to keep in excellent condition by partaking largely of the good things intended for our use, which he purloined in a daring and impudent manner, and devoured when alone and at leisure. Not content with secreting the choicest articles, he made so serious an impression even on the bare necessaries of life, that we were not unfrequently kept on short allowance.

On one occasion we detected him in the very act of concealing some ducks, eggs, and honey, which we knew beforehand had been sent him for our consumption; and we taxed him with the robbery to his face. Ebo, however, disclaimed the imputation with earnestness, and maintained his innocence with considerable volubility. On our entrance he held a bottle of rum in one hand, to which he had been evidently paying his devotions, whilst the other was occupied in shuffling something under a mat. It was no doubt the eunuch's intention to take another draught of the inspiring liquid, whilst thus employed, but, mistaking the hand in which it was held, he snatched the other from underneath the mat, and had actually the head of our duck in his mouth, instead of the bottle, before the error was discovered. This it was which he had taken so much pains to hide from our sight, and the ludicrous misconception of the fellow caused us infinite diversion. As for the eunuch, he was not the least disconcerted; and although we discovered the honey and eggs also concealed in another part of his house, he roundly asserted that he had purchased them at the market the day before. Complaints were made to the king of his conduct, without producing a beneficial effect upon the gormandizing Ebo, who continued to feed without mercy on our provisions, while his paunch maintained its usual enviable state of rotundity and bulk, at the expense of our empty stomachs.

Captain Clapperton diverted the people of

Katunga by a display of rockets at different times; this was the only means we had of making ourselves in the least degree the instruments of pleasure to them in return for their good nature; and this they appeared to enjoy with all the zest that a novelty generally inspires in the breasts of savages, even after it had ceased to be a novelty. At first the spectators were terrified with the exhibition, but familiarity with it soon wore off that impression, and they never appeared satisfied with gazing at our artificial fire-works. The inhabitants, on their part, with their sovereign at their head, endeavoured to prolong our stay with them by straining every nerve to please, and beguiled the time by all the amusements they could think of. Amongst other allurements held out by Mansolah towards this end, that of seeing him *as a king*, which would shortly be the case, was repeatedly urged with much warmth. "You behold me now, only as a poor man," observed his majesty, "but by and by I shall be a king indeed."

A womanish fondness for dress and admiration, and a childish vanity in the most trivial as well as more important concerns, were strikingly visible in the character of every prince we met with in Africa; nor did the monarch of Yariba think these frivolities beneath him, any more than his royal neighbours; but in his case there was mixed up with this weakness, a certain consciousness of the absurdity of it, which I never observed in the character of any other African whatever. Mansolah only conformed to the whims and fancies of his people, he said, when he attired himself so fancifully; for that they preferred a ruler with a smart and gorgeous exterior, even if he happened to be the most odious tyrant on the face of the earth, to a prince meanly dressed, although he were endowed with every amiable quality. It was not, therefore, in compliance with his own inclination that he had accepted, with so great apparent satisfaction, the trinkets we had given him for the adornment of his person, but solely to please his subjects, to whose taste he always accommodated himself. Against these philosophical expressions of the Sultan of Yariba, however, his conduct and actions sadly militated, for he smiled with delight on beholding a brass watch-chain he had received of us; his eyes sparkled with rapture at the sight of a gold-headed cane Captain Clapperton had offered for his acceptance; while a necklace of large handsome coral beads positively threw him into a transport of joy.

The same eager curiosity that had been displayed on the road from Badagry, was evinced by the people of Katunga; but there was no boldness, no impudence, no daring effrontery, with the latter; they every where made way for us to pass, when either curiosity or the desire of exercise induced us to walk through their town, or its environs, and retreating to a short distance, made a profound obeisance, and in some cases even went so far as to prostrate themselves in the dust before us, although these were acts of humiliation we never countenanced nor approved of. The more respectable part of the inhabitants, on meeting with us in the streets, used to run up to shake hands, with as much cordiality as if they had known us from our childhood; and would very kindly enquire after our healths, not merely for the sake of having something to say, as is the case in England, but prompted by an interest and concern they could not disguise. We felt assured that their motive for asking sprang from a sincere desire of *knowing*, in order that they might sympathise with us if we were ill, or congratulate us if we enjoyed tolerable health.

The strong desire Mansolah felt and expressed for us to remain at least for a few months with him, made that prince guilty, on more than one occasion, of dissimulation, and even falsehood, —which detracts greatly from his merit, for in other respects he was a generous, sensible, good natured man. He was fruitful in expedients against our setting out, and used every means that ingenuity could suggest, to counteract our intentions of prosecuting our journey; at one time alleging that the Falatahs, (who had joined a party in a civil war that was then raging in Nyffé, between two princes, who were disputing the right of succession to their deceased father's throne,) intercepted all communication between that country, through which it was our intention to pass, and Yariba, or rather Katunga, its capital;

and at another time asserting that he had sent messengers to Yarro, one of his own provinces, to ascertain whether the road was clear in that direction; for he was determined, he said, not to be instrumental towards our falling into the hands of the Falatahs. His assertion, with regard to the war in Nyffé, proved indeed to be correct; but for some indefinable reason, besides those adduced, he was excessively jealous of our having the least intercourse with the Falatahs, his most inveterate enemies, who, as he repeatedly and feelingly expressed himself, "had torn down his father's house."

Amongst the amusements of the inhabitants of Katunga, dancing and tumbling hold a prominent rank. With respect to the latter diversion, they cannot be excelled by any people in the world; their evolutions in the air are perfectly astonishing, and by the suppleness and pliability of their limbs, by their bending, and turning, and twisting themselves into all manner of shapes, one would be almost inclined to believe that they have not a single bone in their bodies.

During our stay at Katunga we were witnesses to a kind of pantomime, which amusement the inhabitants generally prefer, in honor of the caboceers, whenever they pay a visit to the king, as was the case in that instance. The place chosen for the exhibition was a large enclosure, contiguous to the king's residence, covered with verdure, and as level as a bowling-green. It was rendered particularly pleasant by the refreshing shade afforded by clumps of tall trees, which studded the spot in all directions. Two huge shapeless rocks of crumbling granite marked the limits of the play-ground to the south; the king's house those to the north; and a range of trees intercepted the view to the east and west. A lofty fan-palm-tree grew in the centre of the place, under the branches of which the actors were accommodated; and a temporary fence, erected round its trunk, screened them from observation, whenever they chose to remain concealed.

A most astounding din from drums, horns, and whistles, was the signal for the performers to begin their manœuvres. The first act consisted of dancing, capering, and tumbling by about twenty men, enveloped in sacks, which novel and elegant divertisement was continued with admirable spirit for a full half hour, when the contents of the sacks becoming fatigued, bundled themselves back to the palm-tree.

The second act commenced almost immediately after, with attempting to catch the *boa constrictor*. To effect this object, one of the dancing sacks came out of the place of its concealment, and fell gently and most conveniently to the ground, when a monstrous mishapen figure, with a head-dress resembling in size and shape a common English wash-tray, from which streamed a variety of strips of scarlet damask and country cloth, slowly approached the recumbent sack from behind the fence. The figure was of most gigantic stature, and changed its appearance as often as the enchanted Turk in our puppet-shows. It held in its hand a sword, and by its motions, as well as the commanding attitude it assumed over the other actors, appeared to be the director of the pageant. Another fellow in a sack was then brought out, and being placed bolt upright by the side of the figure, by the application of a slight blow, fell near to its peaceable companion, and by a little shifting contrived to get its head close to that of the other. The mouths of the two sacks having been previously unsewn, the contents of the one crawled into the other, and after these formalities the representation of the boa presently began. The reptile at first thrust its head out of the bag and attempted to lay hold of the tremendous figure, who contrived, dexterously enough, to make it draw itself into the sack again by a flourish of his weapon, which the knowing animal appeared to understand perfectly well. The head of the boa was then jutted out in a different direction, and by degrees the whole body protruded itself from the place of its confinement into open day light, and remained exposed for a few seconds to the gaze of the multitude. It appeared to be about fourteen feet in length, and by reason of the painted cloth with which it was covered, might easily be mistaken for the animal it was intended to represent. The angry monster, after a short pause, pursued the fantastical figure with the sword, rather slowly, to be sure, but withal very naturally—going through the motions of a snake by coiling itself round like a rope, opening and shutting its jaws, and darting out its forked tongue; all of which elicited the rapturous applauses of the bystanders. But the pursued, although it never was at a greater distance from the reptile than a few feet, never had the courage to come in contact with its fangs. At length, at a given signal by the manager, the whole troop of actors rushed to the spot; they were then sackless, but their features were effectually concealed by masks reaching to the bosom. The figure then began to act on the offensive, by chopping the irritated monster's tail with his weapon in a shocking and most unmerciful manner. The snake apparently writhed in agony, and convulsively twisting its body for a few moments, whilst it endeavoured, without effect, to be revenged on its formidable adversary by extending its neck to bite; when life seeming to be nearly extinguished, it was borne off on the shoulders of the actors to the fetish-house.

The third and last part of this extraordinary ceremony, consisted in the representation of the caricature of a white man. One of the sack-dancers, placed by himself on a clear spot of ground, near to the palm-tree, gradually detached his covering, and exposed the figure of a man, of a chalky whiteness, to the fixed looks of the people, who set up so terrific a shout of approbation that it startled us, prepared as we had been to expect some such explosion. The figure walked but indifferently well, and mimicked our actions as badly; the composition with which it was bedaubed, evidently preventing the actor from using his limbs freely, or performing his part with the facility he could have wished; although his embarrassment was apparent to us, yet the populace did not seem to take the least notice of this defect, and an universal roar of laughter expressed the delight which filled every bosom. The pantomimic incident had now attained its utmost bounds, and all eyes, swimming in tears, were directed first to us, and then to the intended representation of us, as much as to say, "what a faithful and striking resemblance!" We entered most cordially into the good humour of the moment, not so much on account of the clumsy and unsightly figure before us, as to see a vast circle of white teeth grinning at the same moment, and producing an irresistibly ludicrous effect. After exhibiting himself in this manner about an hour, the white man was enveloped in his sack, and borne, like the serpent, to the fetish-house, when the amusements ended, and the people quietly dispersed. Between the acts we were entertained with a concert of drums and whistles, as well as country songs from the females who were present, in the choruses of which the people generally joined.

The Yarro messengers, of whom Mansolah had spoken, having returned, and given a favorable report of the state of the roads, on Monday the 6th of March, we bade adieu to Katunga, its ruler, and inhabitants, and pursued our journey, attended by the same escort that had conducted us into the city. Mr. Houtson was left behind, and returned to the coast, where he was almost immediately seized with fever, and expired after an illness of only a few days. Our party was therefore reduced to two Europeans only, my master and myself.

We passed through several villages which had been pillaged and burnt by the Falatahs, on the following and three successive days; and on the 11th we arrived at a mean dirty-looking village, remarkable only as being the first in the Borghoo country.

The huts of the inhabitants are constructed in a circular form, after the Bornou fashion, and their tops ornamented with crocodiles' eggs, considered as an effectual protection against the ravages of those animals, which are much dreaded by all classes, but with what justice I know not. We left the village at four o'clock in the afternoon; and the horse on which I rode being in better condition than the others, I was considerably in advance of the rest of the party, when the animal made a sudden halt, and all my endeavours were inadequate to make him proceed. There he stood like a block of marble, keeping his eyes rivetted on something that was approaching us, and I had scarcely time to consider what it could possibly be, when a fine antelope bounded before me with incredible swiftness, and in the next moment two huge lions, with mane and tail erect, crossed the path but a couple of yards from the horse's head, almost with equal speed, and covered with foam. A tremendous roar, which made the forest tremble, informed me in another minute that the lions had overtaken their prey; but the sudden and unexpected appearance of those ferocious animals startled me as much as it had intimidated the horse before, and I hastened back to the party, my poor beast trembling violently the whole of the way. Fortunately the lions, which were male and female, were so eager in the chase, that both the horse and its rider were unobserved by them; otherwise it might have gone hard with me, for I saw not the slightest chance of escaping. We halted in the woods that night; but fancying every sound I heard was the roaring of a lion, I could not compose myself to sleep. Next day I was severely indisposed, and the party was obliged to stop several times on the road on my account; a languid faintness frequently overpowering me, and rendering me insensible to surrounding objects. We put up at a town called Socka for the night, and on the 13th an escort from the king of Khiama arrived, mounted on excellent horses, little inferior to the English breed; but after delivering their monarch's message, the fellows very unceremoniously began plundering the villagers of goats, pigs, and poultry. The escort consisted of fifty horsemen, bold, fierce-looking fellows, more resembling a desperate band of robbers than peaceably-disposed individuals.

Traversing a pleasant and fertile country, we entered the city of Khiama about ten in the morning, and were immediately conducted to the house of his majesty, whom we found sitting under the porch of his door, chucking some of his young wives under the chin. After shaking hands, he expressed a wish for us to repose ourselves till the heat of the day was over, and said he would pay us a visit in the cool of the evening.

The king redeemed his pledge, and came at the appointed time, riding on one of the handsomest horses I ever saw. He was attended by numbers of people on horseback and on foot, and half a dozen naked girls *circling* round the animal on which he rode, flourishing spears with which they were furnished, and singing, in a loud voice, the praises of their husband and prince. Yarro (that is the monarch's name) dismounted and entered our house, followed by the girls, who had left their weapons outside, and for decency's sake had wrapped a piece of striped cotton round their delicate waists. After an hour's conversation, in the course of which Captain Clapperton informed him of our motives for visiting his country, whither we intended to go, &c. the king left us, infinitely pleased, and the extraordinary procession returned in much the same order as it had come. A few minutes only had elapsed, when we were favored with a visit from the chief of a Houssa gafflee, or caravan (returned the day before from Gonja and Ashantee), and accompanied by a native of Bornou, both of whom strongly advised us to quit Khiama with as little delay as possible, asserting that the inhabitants were thieves to a man, and would not let slip the opportunity of putting their pilfering propensity to the trial on our goods and baggage. The Houssa caravan consisted of about a thousand individuals of both sexes, many of whom traded in the kola or goora nut. This nut, which is in high esteem and general use all through the interior, is frequently applied to the same purpose as the calumet of peace amongst the North American Indians, and is likewise used on all public occasions to testify the good understanding that prevails in the assembly: when presented to private individuals, it signifies that there is peace between the donor and receiver. The kola is the fruit of a beautiful tree, growing in abundance on many parts of the coast, and is an agreeable bitter and astringent; it also produces a rich yellow dye, which is oftentimes used by the natives in the embellishment of their persons. In some districts the nut is exceedingly scarce, and fetches an exhorbitant price; hence the traffic in it is carried on to an incredible extent, and yields an immense profit to those who are venturesome enough to risk the dangers of a long and perilous journey.

Having been provided with a messenger,

carriers, and horses, we quitted Khiama on the 18th, without experiencing, whilst in the city, any of the incoveniences we had been led to apprehend—the Houssa caravan had left us an hour or two previously, to proceed on the same road as ourselves. In the course of the morning we passed through two villages, excessively clean, inhabited by Falatahs, who were chiefly employed in pounding corn in wooden mortars; and sleeping at Bonàga, we overtook the caravan on Sunday the 19th. It was composed of a long line of horsemen, and people of both sexes on foot, loaded with bundles, both men and beasts apparently heartily tired with their long march. The women with them, as in every other instance that came within the compass of our own observation, bore the heaviest burdens, and seemed actually sinking to the earth with heat and fatigue, without exciting the compassion, or obtaining the assistance of the ruder and stronger companions of their journey; although several of the latter had little else to do besides keeping pace with the horses. We slept in a wood, under a tree, for the night, about half a mile from the Gonja traders.

The country travelled over since we had left Katunga differed but slightly from the descriptions which have already been given of the other parts; the soil generally consisting of a rich reddish loam, intermixed with fine gravel. In some places it is thickly wooded, but in others not more than a dozen trees are to be found on an acre of land; on all sides, however, it is highly picturesque and beautiful.

Numerous traces of antelopes, elephants, &c. were observable in the path; but (except in the instance before mentioned) we saw but few of those animals. The natives hunt the former, and with spears and poisoned arrows contrive to procure great numbers of them. The arrow is a speedy and effectual means of destroying wild animals; for being tipped with poison, the wound it inflicts is sure to prove mortal, although not quite so instantaneously as the natives would make one believe. The flesh of antelopes slain in this manner is eaten with avidity by the people, the hunters simply cutting off the parts near which the arrow may happen to penetrate. When this vegetable poison is taken internally it produces no pernicious effects, and it is only when it mingles with the blood that its consequences are so fatal. The natives, who, like the vulgar in Europe, are fond of the wonderful, tell a thousand singular stories respecting its malignancy, which are too improbable and ridiculous to be believed.

At Barakina, a small but pleasant village, we met a hunter, clad in a leopard's skin, returning from the chase, with his bow and arrows slung on his shoulder, and a light spear in his hand; a man with a dead antelope followed at a little distance; and three panting hounds, whose tongues, lolling out of their mouths, betrayed the severity of the exercise they had undergone, came after the man. The sable Nimrod took not the least notice of us, but passed through the village as incuriously as if he had been in the habit of seeing white faces every day.

At twelve at noon on the same day we crossed a river said to take its rise in Nyffé, and to flow into the Niger above Rakah. Alligators were plentiful in the river, and one of our carriers, who was sent to fetch a calabash of water, was pursued by one of these monsters almost up to the trees under which our little party was encamped. The poor fellow was terribly frightened, and out of breath, on approaching us; and not all the promises in the world could induce him to make a second visit to the river.

Our ears were ravished by the warbling of hundreds of small birds, which, with parrots and parroquets, peopled the branches of the trees in the vicinity of the stream, whose delightful banks were thereby overshadowed; and the eye was incessantly saluted with a variety of beautiful objects—groves of noble trees, verdant hills, and smiling plains, through which the river winded, carrying fertility and beauty in its course, and altogether forming a rich and charming landscape.

We slept at Billa, a village on the south side of the river, in the night; and on the morning of Tuesday an escort of four horsemen arrived from the chief, or King of Wow Wow, to conduct us to that city, where we arrived after a journey of four hours, and took our station outside the monarch's house, till its royal inmate, who was dressing to receive us, should make his appearance. After putting our patience to a severe trial, the King at length came out, supported on a staff, and walking with the solemn pace of a Spaniard up to our tree, seated himself on a stool that had been previously placed there for that purpose. We then dismounted, but were sorely dismayed on observing the chief, contrary to the custom of the country, shrinking from our hands which were extended towards him, just with as much repugnance as a European would from the proffered hand of a leper; but it was only to cover his with his tobe, which being done, he shook hands with the utmost cordiality. The King being a Mohammedan, fancied that the touch of a Christian would defile him; but this stiffness wore off on a more familiar acquaintance, and he subsequently displayed the characteristic virtues of Africans—generally hospitality and benevolence.

In the evening we were visited by fifteen Dahomans, who saluted us with a discharge from two old rusty muskets. These men had been for five months beforehand assisting the Sultan of Youri in his war with the Falatahs, and were so far on their return to their own country. They extolled to the skies their own prowess in their engagements with the Falatahs, whilst they represented the people of Youri as the greatest cowards in the world. We were informed by them that Niki, five days' journey from Khiama, is the most considerable city in Borghoo; and that it was only about fifteen or sixteen days' journey from Abomey, the capital of Dahomy.

Wow Wow is the metropolis of a province of the same name, in the empire of Borghoo, and is governed by a ruler, named Mohammed, a Mussulman, strongly addicted to superstition, but of mild, unassuming, and pleasing manners. The city lies on a beautiful rising ground, with gentle hills on every side; and may contain, on a hasty computation, perhaps twenty thousand inhabitants. It is surrounded by a high and substantial mud wall, and broad deep trench. The houses in it are circular, and the streets spacious and airy; and it is without exception the neatest, most wholesome, and best regulated town of any in the interior. The inhabitants, or at least the better sort of them, dress in tobes, caps, and trousers; and are a cheerful, thoughtless set of people, yet fonder of music, carousing, singing, and dancing, than any people we met with in Africa. Drunkenness is their besetting sin; and the beverage in most esteem with them is a species of ale, called *pitto*, obtained from Indian corn previously made into malt. The process is simple, being much the same as the brewing of beer in England; only no hops are added to the malt.

This sad propensity to intoxication, which males and females in every *grade* of society love to cultivate, is the agent of many irregularities, and cause their notions of morality to be so very lax, that chastity itself is barely acknowledged by them as an excellence; nevertheless the people of Wow Wow have many substantial virtues, and agreeable qualities, which one can hardly help loving them for. Their generous hospitality is unbounded, and a parcel of more merry, facetious, happy scoundrels than the generality of them is not to be found in the world.

The soil in the neighbourhood of Wow Wow is surprisingly rich and heavy; so that many of the necessaries of life spring up almost spontaneously from the earth, and others require but trifling labour in their cultivation and general management; hence the people have abundance of leisure, which they employ in feasting, drinking, sleeping, visiting, and oftentimes in less innocent recreations than these.

The direct road from Badagry, Gonja, Dahomy, Ashantee, Jannah — to Nyffée, Houssa, Bornou, &c. lying through the town, its inhabitants are supplied with many of the luxuries of life at a more reasonable rate than their countrymen in less frequented districts, and their habitations have consequently more pretensions to *comfort* than those of any people between Badagry and Soccasoo.

Articles of merchandise, of English manufacture, such as Manchester goods, pewter plates, jugs, and dishes, are very common, both in Khiama and Wow Wow; and it is really laughable to observe to what elegant uses some of the latter are applied.

The religion is either idolatry or Islamism; but these are so blended into each other, that it would be difficult to draw a line of distinction between the professors of either faith. Bigotry is unknown, and the wildest doctrines are tolerated with an amiable and forbearing spirit that does the government infinite credit!

The marriages of the people are exceedingly simple, differing in no essential particular from the manner in which that ceremony is practised amongst Africans generally. A pagan pays his addresses to a girl, and if, after a short acquaintance, he fancies she will answer his purpose, he simply gives or sends a small present to the parents, who rarely raise any obstacles to balk his wishes; whereupon the female quits her father's house, and resides, as long as she lives, with her suitor. The courtship of a Mohammedan is carried on in much the same fashion, with the addition of reading the *fatha* (marriage ceremony). When tired of each other the "fatha" is again read, and the couple part for ever, (although they may have lived together for twenty years,) with as much coolness and unconcern as if they had been utter strangers to each other. This *convenient* custom is greatly relished by every one, and is seldom known to produce any unpleasant consequences.

The Africans have less of *sentiment* in their love affairs than Europeans; they have no stolen interviews—no rambling in verdant fields—no affectionate squeezes of the hand—no language of the eyes—no refined feeling—no moonlight reveries; all is conducted in the most unpoetical business-like way imaginable, and is considered in the light of one of their least important concerns; the lover merely saying to his intended bride, " Should you like to become my wife, my dear?" to which the lady replies, " I have no objection." " Then come and live with me," retorts the man; and from that hour the couple reside together. This is the beginning and end of their courtship, and I never heard of a refusal on the lady's part to embrace the proposal. The notions of female perfection amongst the people consist in the bulk, plumpness, and rotundity of the object; and a perfect beauty in their estimation, as it has often been remarked, is " a load for a camel!" This delicacy of taste is as general in Africa as it is in Turkey in Europe, although I never heard that the natives of the former country use any artificial means of increasing the size of their daughters, in order to their obtaining admirers. Allowing the qualities of bulk, &c. to be the criterion of beauty, the widow Zuma, who will by and by be introduced, would bear away the palm of superiority from every competitor, that lady being a whole world of fat and loveliness! and consequently the most elegant, the most charming, the most graceful, the most amiable, the most captivating beauty in the continent of Africa!!

The ideas of handsomeness entertained by the *fair* sex, with regard to their male companions, are extremely vague, and it is even difficult to ascertain whether they have any notion of comeliness at all; for a lady eagerly embraces the first offer, even if the fellow that makes it be as old as Methusala, and ugly as Sin. As a proof of this, I knew a pretty girl at Wow Wow, blooming with youth, and full of life and spirit, possessing besides uncommon shrewdness for an African: to this individual a tall, lanky, phantom-like man, evidently tottering on the brink of the grave, whose lantern jaws were of a truly formidable length, and who squinted most divinely, offered himself, and was of course accepted, although he had upwards of twenty wives at the time. On my questioning the damsel as to the reasons of her acceptance of a person so excessively old and ugly as her spouse, she answered very smartly something equivalent to the ancient saying still in use amongst the lower class of people in England, " a toad is a pearl in a duck's eye! " and instantly left me. No doubt the number of wives of the old gentleman, which in Europe would be considered as a serious grievance, was one of the principal motives that had swayed her in the choice she had made; as by that criterion the wealth of the party is judged of.

When a husband dies; the wives who have not borne him children are sold; whereas those who have had that good fortune are free for life, or at least till they change their condition a second time. The widows wear a rope round their head, neck, and waist, as mourning for their deceased husbands, for the space of twelve months (if they find no one inclined to make them an offer before the expiration of that period), when their weeds are flung off, and they cheerfully resume their ordinary apparel.

When a Borghoo man dies, a pit is dug, either in his own house, or very near to it, and the body is placed in a sitting posture, with the hands and feet tied tightly with cord; the head inclining upwards. The horse and dog of the deceased, after being slaughtered, are buried with him, to assist him in his peregrinations in the other world; and his spear, and bow and arrows, are placed over the grave for the same purpose. On my questioning an inhabitant of Wow Wow, how it was possible for a man so confined to mount the horse, he shook his head, as much as to say the subject was of too sacred and delicate a nature to be talked lightly of.

The men of Wow Wow are, in most instances, tall and well formed, and the women handsome, having far greater pretensions to beauty than either the people of Yariba, or those of Khiama, a neighbouring state. Numbers of horses are kept by the Wow-Wownese, the finest of which are imported from Bornou; the native breed, although strong and spirited, being excessively small. Horned cattle are much finer, and their flesh is superior in quality to those found on the coast. They are bred principally by Falatahs, numerous tribes of whom are scattered over the face of the country.

Some of these same Falatahs profess the Mahommedan faith, and some worship idols, like the natives themselves, whilst others have no outward form of religion at all. Many of them are for ever wandering from place to place, like the Bedouin Arabs, and others spend a tranquil existence in the occupations of pasturage and agriculture. Several are suspected of stirring up the minds of the people against their rulers, and treated accordingly with as much contumely and disrespect as the Jews in some countries of Europe; and others again contribute, in an essential degree, to the comforts and convenience of the community in whose towns they may happen to dwell, and by whom they are esteemed and caressed; but all have less simplicity in their manners, and infinitely more art in their dealings, than those of the negro cast of feature, and, to every appearance, are a stage further advanced in civilization than they.

Boussa is a province contiguous to Wow Wow, whose capital is also called Boussa, and is but one day's journey, or about twenty miles, from the latter place. The island of Boussa, on which the city is built, is about three miles in length, and little more than one in breadth. It is situated in the river Niger, or, more properly speaking, the Quorra, and is chiefly remarkable as the place where the enterprising Mr. Park and his companions came by their melancholy death. It may contain sixteen or eighteen thousand inhabitants. The road to it from Wow Wow in the dry season is excellent, but in the wet or rainy months is almost impassable, by reason of its proximity to the river, which oftentimes overflows its banks. The country between the two capitals is hilly, woody, and picturesque, rivalling in beauty any portion between Badagry and Soccatoo; and its most remarkable feature is a rocky mountain in the shape of a cone, which Captain Clapperton called, after the reigning Monarch of England, " Mount George."

Thick woods approach even to the margin of the Quorra, and are tenanted by an ancient tribe of people termed Cumbrie (or Cumbrians), by all accounts the aborigines of the country, a harmless stupid race, who, from their tractable dispositions and love of tranquillity, are frequently imposed on by their spirited and more artful neighbours, and sold into slavery whenever a favourable opportunity can be obtained of kidnapping them.

Many heavy branches of trees overhang, and, as it were, embrace the Menài, a branch of the Quorra, as it flows by, and impart a darkness and melancholy to the spot which are any thing but agreeable or enlivening. It was nearly sunset when I got into the canoe, in which I was ferried across the stream to Boussa; the evening was calm, clear, and beautiful; the fire-fly had already begun to shine and buzz in the air; the hollow roar of the crocodile was heard from the borders of the current, and the declining sun had tinged the surface of the water with a rich hue of crimson. The sound of sweet-toned instruments, and the hum of human voices mingling in concert, and wafted from the city to which I was approaching, produced a soothing and delightful effect; and as the little bark was propelled slowly through the lazy stream, the music sounded like a symphony of angels' voices floating from the skies.

The owner of the boat pointed out the spot where my daring countrymen had so unfortunately perished. After quitting it, their canoe had drifted on a reef of sunken rocks, not more than half a stone's throw from the island, and had gone to pieces.

Numerous small islands jut up from the bosom of the Quorra, which, near Boussa, branches into three distinct streams; but they are uninhabited, and little better than naked rocks. Two of the above streams flow sluggishly onwards, whilst the other rolls with a rapid current, fretting and foaming over vast masses of stone, and creates a noise which at a little distance might be mistaken for that produced by the waving of a forest of tall trees, when agitated by the wind.

The Sultan of Youri, understanding that we intended visiting Boussa, had sent a messenger to that place a week before our arrival there, (with seven canoes laden with provisions,) to conduct us to the capital of his empire; but reports from various quarters agreed in representing the Prince of Youri to be a cruel, treacherous, and wicked man; and this fact, combined with the advanced state of the season, succeeded in deterring Captain Clapperton from embracing the monarch's offer. He told the messenger, however, that it was solely on account of the rainy season so soon setting in, that he was obliged to decline his Sovereign's proposal, but that he would certainly pay him a visit on his return from Bornou.

We had all along been buoyed up with the hope of being able to obtain the journal and papers of the late Mungo Park at Boussa; but, to our great mortification and disappointment we discovered, that they had been either destroyed, or conveyed no one could tell whither, many years before. The inhabitants were exceedingly reserved on the subject of the fatal catastrophe, and uniformly gave equivocating or evasive answers to our enquiries as to the manner in which it had occurred. They seemed indeed overwhelmed with shame at the part they or their fathers had taken in the dreadful tragedy, and did all in their power to shift the blame from the shoulders of themselves and their countrymen.

The following appeared the most accurate and best authenticated version of the dismal story of the deaths of Park and Martin, that I was enabled to obtain whilst I was in the country:

The voyagers had reached Youri in safety, and were on intimate and familiar terms with its Sultan, father to the reigning prince, who intreated them to finish their journey through the country by land, instead of proceeding down the Quorra to the salt water; observing, that the people inhabiting the islands and borders of the river, were ferocious in their manners, and would not suffer their canoe to proceed without having first rifled it of its contents, and exposed them to every species of indignity and insult; and that if their lives were spared, they would infallibly be detained as domestic slaves. This evil report was considered as the effect of jealousy and prejudice: and, disregarding the prudent counsel of the Sultan of Youri, the ill-fated adventurers proceeded down the Quorra as far as the island of Boussa, from whence their strange-looking anoe was observed by one or two of the inhabitants, whose shouts brought numbers of their companions, armed with bows and arrows, to the spot. At that time the usurpations of the Falatahs had begun to be the general talk of the black population of the country, so that the people of Boussa, who had only *heard* of that warlike nation, fancied Mr. Park and his associates to be some of them, coming with the intention of taking their town, and subjugating its inhabitants. Under this impression, they saluted the unfortunate Englishmen from the beach with showers of missiles and poisoned arrows, which were returned by the latter with a discharge of musketry. A small white flag had been previously waved by our countrymen, in token of their peaceable intentions; but this symbol not being understood by the people of Boussa, they continued firing arrows, till they were joined by the whole male population of the island, when the unequal contest was renewed with greater violence than ever. In the meantime the Englishmen, with the blacks they had with them, kept firing unceasingly amongst the multitude on shore, killing many, and wounding a still greater number, till their ammunition being expended, and seeing every hope of life cut off, they threw their goods overboard; and desiring their sable assistants to swim towards the beach, locked themselves firmly in each other's arms, and springing into the water, instantly sank, and were never seen again.

The bodies of the two slaves, who attempted to save their lives by swimming, were pierced with a grove of arrows, but they subsequently recovered from the effects of their wounds, and were certainly alive when we were at Boussa, but, as I understood afterwards, they were carefully concealed, in order to prevent our making any inquiries of them relative to the affair.

Resistance being thus at an end, the floating property had been eagerly laid hold of by the people of Boussa, and taken in triumph to their city. In the evening they formed a circle round it, and for several days and nights nothing was to be seen or heard but feasting and rejoicing; but it happened that before their revelries were well over, an infectious disease, whereof they had not previously had the most distant idea, raged in the island, and swept off the Sultan, with numbers of his subjects; and it was remarked, that those who had been most active in the destruction of the strangers were cut off to a man, expiring in great agony. The people endeavoured to appease the wrath of the white man's God, (by whose instrumentality they were firmly persuaded the destroying plague had reached them,) by the offering of sacrifices, and afterwards by setting fire to all the articles found on the surface of the water; shortly after which, it is asserted, the pestilence left the island. Meantime the news of the occurrence, and its fatal results, spread like wild-fire through the neighbouring states; and the people of Boussa were stigmatized with a reproachful epithet, for having been guilty of so heinous a crime. Hence the studied reserve of the reigning Sultan and his subjects, which no consideration could tempt them to break through, so as to enter into the details of the tragedy; and hence also the expression, so beneficial to us in those regions, and so prevalent amongst all ranks and conditions: " Do not hurt the white men; for if you do, you *will perish like the people of Boussa!*"

CHAPTER VI.

Widow Zuma's love adventures—Departure from Wow Wow—Arrival at Coulfo—Civil war in Nyffé—Ceremonies observed by the people of Coulfo at the end of the Rhamadan—Tornado at that place, and its disastrous consequences—The Travellers quit Coulfo, and proceed on their journey—The Author attacked with dysentery—His sufferings—Noble conduct of Captain Clapperton towards him—They enter Zeg Zeg—Arrive at Kano.

WHILST we remained in the city of Wow Wow, we were visited almost every day by a widow lady, of Arab extraction, named *Zuma* (*Honey* in English), between thirty and forty years of age, who, if one might be allowed to judge from the remaining charms which were still visible in her countenance, had been really beautiful in her younger years. This individual was vastly rich, being the acknowledged mistress of a thousand slaves; and from her excescessive plumpness, and extraordinary size, was the exact counterpart of our bulky friend Ebo, the fat eunuch of Katunga. Zuma's affection for my master and myself was unbounded, and as it led to an adventure perhaps never equalled in novelty by any incident that has occurred to Europeans in the bosom of Africa, I hope I may be forgiven in attempting to trace its causes and effects, without which my narrative would be incomplete; for they are so intimately connected with each other, that it would be impossible to disunite them.

In order to give a clearer idea of the story, it will be necessary to remark, that Zuma was married in early life to one of the principal inhabitants of Wow Wow; but her spouse dying shortly after she had given birth to a son, she was left immensely rich, and lived in almost regal splendour in the native town of her deceased husband. Nature had endowed Zuma with an active, restless, and ambitious mind; insomuch that not long after she had become a widow, and before the regular term of mourning had expired, her weeds were thrown aside, and she aspired to the government of Wow Wow, by attempting to depose her sovereign. But Mohammed, although an imbecile and superstitious prince, could

"Bear, like a Turk, no rival near his throne!"

and was roused into action at the threatening aspect his too powerful subject had assumed. Instantly arming his vassals, he made a sudden and unexpected attack on the slaves of the rebellious lady, who for want of an efficient leader were put completely to the rout, though without bloodshed, and Zuma herself taken prisoner. Whether it was owing to the profound veneration in which that elegant lady's charms were held by the monarch, to the natural mildness of his disposition, or to the fear of stirring up the people against him, I could not learn; but certain it is that Zuma was pardoned, and set at liberty, after a confinement of only one or two days; and though she had repeated her treasonable attempt several times, even up to the period of our visiting the city, the same amiable forbearance had been extended to her.

It was the misfortune of the far-famed Zuma

to fancy herself, for no reason in the world, to be extremely fair, and although she had certainly passed the " Age of the Passions," she took it into her head to fall desperately in love with me, whose complexion, she affirmed, rivalled her own in whiteness! The frequency of her visitations to our house nourished the tender feeling, which was encouraged by Captain Clapperton, who relished a joke with all his heart, and did his utmost to inflame the lady's passion, by passing a thousand unmeaning compliments on the regularity of my features, and the handsomeness of my person. " See what beautiful eyes he has," observed the Captain; " if you were to search from Badagry to Wow Wow, and from Wow Wow to Bornou, you would not find such eyes." For my own part I was but a novice in the art of courtship, and imagining it to be altogether in jest, took little pains to spoil the fun by shrinking from it. Besides, Zuma had behaved remarkably well to us in sending, repeatedly, presents of provisions, together with every luxury with which she was acquainted, and I was rather glad than otherwise to have her for our guest,

> "For the heart must
> Leap kindly back to kindness;"

and neither of us wished to offend a lady of her consequence by being morose and unsociable in manners, or by repelling her advances with ridicule and contempt.

For an hour together the widow would gaze intently on me, while the most amorous glances shot from her large, full, and certainly beautiful eye, which confused and disconcerted me not a little, even though I was surrounded by strangers and in the heart of Africa; for I had been a wanderer from my childhood, and had had but few opportunities of mingling in the delightful company of the gentler sex in my own country, and consequently was excessively bashful on coming in contact with ladies, whether in the country of the Hottentots, or the birth-place of the widow Zuma.

As for my master, he was sensibly delighted with these interviews, and with his arms folded on his breast, while thick volumes of tobacco-smoke rolled from his pipe, he with the most impenetrable gravity enjoyed the scene, and looked as happy and as much at home as if he had been seated by his friends in his native Scotland. After the widow's departure, it was his usual custom, tapping me on the shoulder, to ask how I felt my heart, and observe what a boast I could make, on our return to England, of so magnificent a conquest.

All this I took in good part for some days; but things beginning, at length, to wear a more serious aspect than I had at first anticipated, I was resolved to bring this whimsical courtship to a conclusion as speedily as possible. I was the more inclined to do so, because I did not wish to wound the feelings of even a *black* lady (for black she most certainly was, although not quite so deep a sable as the aborigines), by trifling with them; nor did I forget the exclamation of the frog in the fable:—" It may be sport to you, but it is death to us!"

Independently of the delicate state of my health, which incapacitated me from carrying on so curious an amour with the spirit and gallantry it required, I was positively afraid that, from the warmth and energy of Zuma's embraces, I should actually be pressed to death between her monstrous arms! I was but a youth, and my short residence in the country had certainly impaired a constitution originally robust and vigorous; by reason of which I was sadly apprehensive that one of her Brobdignagian hugs would send me into the other world with very little ceremony. These reflexions I had seriously revolved in my mind; and on her next visit I candidly told the widow by signs, words, and gestures, that I could not love her; but she either did not or would not understand me. I remarked that I should never choose a *black* wife: she pointed to her face, and said she was a *white* woman. I then observed that it would be impossible for me to exist in her country, the heat being insupportable. Her reply was disinterested and tender:—" Then I will quit it, and follow you to whichever part of the world you may be inclined to lead me to." Thus beset on all sides, I hardly knew what to say next; but after a short pause, summing up all my resolution, I gave my greasy inamorata a flat refusal to see her again in the light of a lover, as it was out of her power to awaken in my breast a corresponding sensation to that which reigned in her own! and saying this I instantly left the apartment; whilst Zuma, poor lady,

> —" Rais'd a sigh so piteous and profound,
> As it did seem to shatter all her bulk,
> And end her being!"

I was surprised, however, to find that my cruelty had produced no visible impression on the widow, and that her *heart* was big in proportion to the largeness of her *body;* for I discovered that she could love *two* individuals at the same time with as much ardour and sincerity as *one* only. Seeing all hopes of success effectually shut out on my side, she had the good sense to discontinue her solicitations (although she continued her kindness), and looked as tenderly on me as ever; and applied herself strenuously to be on a more affectionate and familiar footing with Captain Clapperton, whose favourable notice she strove to attract by all the fascinating allurements she was mistress of; and actually went so far as to bribe Pasko, our Houssa interpreter, with a young and handsome girl for a wife, in order that he might use his *powerful* influence to bring the matter between my master and herself to an amicable adjustment. The old libertine accepted the present with rapture, which made the third or fourth spouse he had had since leaving Badagry, but he was prudent enough to retain his counsel within his own bosom.

A white husband and happiness were synonymous terms with the gentle and delicate Zuma, and she grasped at even the shadow of it with an eagerness and determination that caused her to overstep the boundaries of that amiable modesty which is so pleasing and peculiar a characteristic of her sex, whereby she did more towards injuring her own cause than coyness or reserve would have done. The Captain carried on the innocent game for some time, for we were greatly in want of something to enliven us; and so romantic an adventure as this, in such a place, and under such circumstances, caused us very many hours of diversion, and was an amusing subject of conversation even up to the period of my master's last illness at Soccatoo.

Poor widow Zuma! I almost fancy I see her now, waddling into our house, a moving world of flesh, " puffing and blowing like a blacksmith's bellows," and the very pink and essence of African fashion. Her hair used to be carefully dyed with indigo, and of a rich and vivid blue; her feet and hands stained with hennah and an extraction of the goora-nut, produced alternate streaks of red and yellow; and her teeth were also tinged with a delicate crimson stain. In the adornment of her person, likewise, the buxom widow evinced considerable taste. Her bared neck and bosom were ornamented with coral and gold beads, which, contrasted with the dingy colour of her skin, occasioned a truly captivating effect! while a dress of striped silk, hanging in graceful folds from the waist to the ancles, set off her *fairy form* to the best possible advantage! Thus beautified, the accomplished Zuma used to sit cross-legged on our mat, and chewing the goora-nut, or a little tobacco-snuff, she was without exception the most ravishing object that came across our path in all our wanderings!

One day she invited my master to visit her at her own house, where she took the opportunity of displaying to him her wealth and grandeur, the number of her slaves, and her princely domestic establishment, all of which the tempter assured him he should share with her if he would consent to be her husband. No encouragement whatever was given to the lady; but when Capt. Clapperton left the town for Boussa a short time afterwards, Madam Zuma, dressed in her gaudiest attire, followed when he had got about six miles on his journey, having called before she set out to see me. On this occasion she wore a mantle of silk and gold, and loose trowsers of scarlet silk, with red morocco boots; her blue head was enveloped in the ample folds of a white turban, and she rode astride on the back of a noble horse, which came prancing before the door of our hut, decorated with a number of brass plates and bells, as well as a profusion of charms or amulets enclosed in green, red, and yellow leather. Her saddle-cloth was of scarlet, and the appearance of both widow and horse was singularly imposing. In her train were many spearmen on horseback, and bowmen on foot, with a band of musicians furnished with drums, fiddles, guitars, and flutes, who continued playing till their mistress was fairly out of the town. The widow briefly told me of her intention to accompany Capt. Clapperton to Kano, &c. &c. which eclaircissement startled me for an instant; but, putting on my most serious look, I wished her a pleasant journey, and hoped I should overtake her myself in a day or two. Zuma then took her leave, and the whole cavalcade was quickly out of sight.

I was absolutely longing to learn the issue of this strange elopement of Zuma's; and was engaged in making preparations previously to my departure for Coulfo, in Nyffé, when a message from the king, forbidding my departure from Wow Wow, diverted me from my intention, and overturned all my plans. I had an interview with the irritated Mohammed the same day, and another on the following one; but my efforts to induce him to change his resolution were abortive. He turned a deaf ear to all my eloquence, and would not suffer me to quit the town for any consideration; "For," said the king, "your countryman has eloped with the captious

Zuma, who will raise up enemies, and make war upon me, if she be not speedily checked; and the better way to accomplish this is to detain you here with the baggage, which will bring back the 'great white man,' and the widow will not be able to remain behind long after."

In order to secure me the more effectually, our house was guarded by a dozen soldiers, who had received strict injunctions not to let me escape on any account. I contrived, however, to elude the vigilance of my keepers, and, taking with me a boy only twelve years of age, who had assisted me in making my escape, I hastily mounted my Yariba pony, and was on the road to Boussa in an instant.

At sunset I crossed the Menài, a branch of the Quorra, leading to the island; and after landing shortly entered the city. As soon as I was recognized as one of the strangers, a good house was immediately prepared for my reception, and I was presently honored with a visit from the king and queen, who informed me that my master had left Boussa, and that, if I were to travel all night, it would be impossible to overtake him before the next morning; they would therefore insist upon my remaining and sleeping in the city. My royal visitors staid with me a considerable time, and the queen gave directions about my supper, and even assisted to prepare it with her own hands.

A multitude of the usual questions were put to me by their majesties, which, on account of my almost total ignorance of the language in which they were uttered, I was not very well qualified to answer; but, notwithstanding this inconvenience, we succeeded in making ourselves pretty well understood; and from the excessive kindness, and watchful anxiety to anticipate my wants, displayed by the king and his royal consort, it was evident that I was a great favourite with them.

The queen had certainly not much of the widow Zuma about her, either in appearance or manners; being delicate in person, and possessing a native dignity and gracefulness of mien that could not fail to please. The features of the royal couple bore a closer resemblance to the European than the negro cast, and might be styled handsome, even in England; besides which an ineffable sweetness shone upon the countenance of Medàki, the queen, and there was an agreeableness in the innocent freedom of her deportment that captivated me at first sight. A tear of pity trembled in the expressive eye of Medàki, when, observing my emaciated looks, and surveying me from head to foot, she enquired if I had a mother in my own country; and when I answered that I had not, she said, " Poor white man! then who have you at home to talk about you, and make fetishes for your preservation whilst you remain away?" I was certainly not prepared to meet with such extraordinary kindness at Boussa; and it shows the great revolution that has taken place in the opinions of the people since Mr. Park's appearance in the interior.

I had been extremely unwell before leaving Wow Wow; and my rapid journey on the back of a lean horse, without saddle or bridle, had nowise improved my health; fatigue also had rendered me so sleepy that after supper I could with difficulty keep my eyes open, and my answers to the queries of the royal pair were given at random. It was in vain that I bit my tongue and lips, and used every other means I could devise in order to arouse myself from the stupid state I was in; the inclination to slumber overcame them all, and at last I fell fast asleep. On awaking in the night I found myself alone, with a solitary lamp burning in my apartment; and was informed, an hour or two afterwards, that their majesties, as soon as they saw me fairly insensible, had left me in the care of two slaves, and returned to their own abode, after expressly desiring them to make no noise that might awaken me. Next morning I went to the king to apologize for my unintentional breach of etiquette; and shaking hands with the royal couple, who wished me every happiness, I returned to Wow Wow (whither I had learnt Captain Clapperton had also gone back), in company of two armed men, who had been furnished as a protection against highway robbers, with which the road was declared to be infested. On my arrival in the city, I found that my master had entered it but a few minutes before, but had not seen the fat widow during his absence.

A short time only had elapsed before we resolved to go to the king; and being ushered into an apartment, found the important personage yawning from the effects of his afternoon's nap. The Captain was the fittest person in the world to deal with the African rulers. The first thing he did was to shake hands affectionately and heartily with the sullen Mohammed, covering his face at the same time with smiles and looks of joy on seeing him again; but the king accepted the compliment with just so good a grace as a growling mastiff would receive the caresses of a person against whom he bears a grudge; neither willing to bite the hand that pats its big head, nor wishing to be altogether on a friendly footing with its suspected friend. "What pleasure it gives me to see you again," said my master; "I have not beheld so handsome a face as yours since leaving the city. I suppose you did not think it safe to send my baggage after me; and am therefore come to fetch it myself. I have seen the king of Boussa, who, with the Medàki, gave so very favorable an account of you, that really I am filled with admiration for your talents and virtues; and am sure there cannot be your equal in the whole country." All this the great man listened to with a deal of attention, and one could perceive plainly enough that the sternness of his features gradually gave place to a softer and kindlier expression; indeed, from the commencement of the above well-timed encomium, a smile overspread his sable countenance which promised the most flattering results. His majesty then, with the utmost dignity, detailed his reasons for the line of conduct he had been obliged to adopt, in consequence of his belief that the Captain and the rebellious Zuma had entered into a conspiracy to usurp his authority; that when their treasonable object should be accomplished, he would be put out of the way, in order that my master might take the reins of government into his own hands. He added that the widow had been guilty of similar unlawful practices before, but had failed in her attempts; and that notwithstanding the lenity with which she had been treated, her thoughts were perpetually employed in devising means for the execution of her ambitious designs; and she had moreover threatened him unceasingly with raising an army to overcome and destroy him. As this was spoken with an air of great solemnity, and towards the latter part of it with emotion, which was plainly evinced by his tears, my master thought proper to disclaim, with correspondent energy and seriousness, the imputations on his own character, by professing himself a total stranger to the widow's movements from the time of his departure from Wow Wow; and as for deposing so powerful a prince as Mohammed, and taking Zuma to wife, such things were altogether beyond his ambition; and he ridiculed the very idea of it. He therefore hoped that the king would no longer refuse his permission for the party under his (Captain Clapperton's) command, to go on immediately, as he had bargained with the chief of the Houssa caravan to convey the goods to Kano, and he was impatiently waiting his arrival at the ferry. The old gentleman, however, was not quite so easily prevailed upon as we had anticipated; and in all probability was smitten with the widow's charms himself; for he declared with firmness, that until the absent lady returned, both my master and myself must abandon all thoughts of proceeding on our journey, or of again leaving Wow Wow. Further cajolery, we knew, would have been superfluous, so we were obliged to make a virtue of necessity, and wait patiently the re-appearance of our affectionate friend, the amiable Zuma. To our infinite joy that circumstance took place on the 5th of April, the day after our conference with the prince; the widow had not been able to meet with the object of her tender solicitude, and hearing that he had re-visited Wow Wow, agreeably to the prediction of Mohammed, returned to that town in much the same order as she had quitted it about a week before, without discovering the slightest symptoms either of disappointment at the ill-success of her jaunt, or fear for having so egregiously offended her sovereign.

Like most of her sex, however, Zuma knew perfectly well how to adapt her conduct to circumstances, and was, moreover, complete mistress of the art of dissimulation and deceit; for no sooner had she entered her own habitation, than her splendid habiliments were instantly thrown aside, and a dress of common country cloth substituted in their stead. Thus meanly attired, she paid her respects to Mohammed in our presence, and saluted him by falling on her knees, with her elbows to the earth, while, supporting her head on the palms of her hands, she shed a whole river of tears. Surely

> " Heav'n gave to woman the peculiar grace
> To spin, to weep, and cully human race."

The great man looked sternly on her at first; but whose heart could be proof against *so much* loveliness in distress, and in that humiliating posture? Anger forsook his brow, as the prince of Wow Wow requested the repentant woman to rise; and simply upbraiding her for disregarding his authority and threatening to subvert his government, he shook hands, and desired her to go her way, but be more cautious of offending him in future. The widow accordingly left the house, and shaking the dust from her feet in token of bravado, cast a "longing, lingering look behind;"—and we saw no more of the generous, the kind-hearted, the affectionate, the ambitious, but above all the enormous widow Zuma!

This singular adventure, although it caused us to laugh heartily, had been of a much more serious nature than we could have foreseen, and had given us much unnecessary trouble, as well as occasioned some days' delay; but when it was thus satisfactorily terminated, we resolved to be more guarded in encouraging, even in jest, the advances of the African belles, as our lives might thereby be endangered, by exciting the prejudices of the people against us. The widow being returned, and having promised to abide in peace, his majesty of Wow Wow offered no further impediment to our departure, and we quitted his capital on the following day.

After passing through three or four insignificant villages, inhabited by *Cambrie*, we arrived at Comoe, a good-sized town, about half a mile from the ferry, in which we remained three days, as Captain Clapperton was too weak and ill to proceed at an earlier period.

On the 10th we crossed the Quorra, running in a southerly direction, which is full of diminutive islands, and about the width of the Thames at Westminster. We had now left the Borghoo country, and were treading on the soil of Nyffé; and notwithstanding the unfavorable account every where received of the rapacity, dishonesty, and injustice of the natives generally, we ever found them strictly honorable in their dealings towards us, good-natured and cheerful; and were always ready not only to do a benevolent action, but willing to sacrifice personal comfort to our accommodation.

At one o'clock we entered Galloway, a village about eight miles from the Quorra, where we changed carriers, and reaching another village called Yowta, slept there for the night. Iron is found in abundance on and in the neighbouring hills, and requires very little labour in procuring it. The plains and borders of the river were cultivated with yams, millet, the plantain, &c. We observed numerous nests of termites (the white ants) at and near Yowta, reared by those formidable insects to the almost incredible height of twenty feet. These immense ant-hills were constructed of earth or clay, divided into distinct apartments, which evinced considerable ingenuity, and at a distance greatly resembled the huts of the natives.

The country traversed was exceedingly populous, and on the eleventh the villages lay at no greater distance from each other than two miles; at every one of which we were obliged to change carriers, and this caused us infini.e trouble and great delay. The chief of the Houssa caravan also began to equivocate, raising a thousand obstacles in our way, and did all in his power to detain us on the road as long as possible, in order that he might avoid the Falatahs, who were then at Coulfo, making preparations for their return to Soccasoo.

On Wednesday the 12th we crossed a stream, over which was thrown a wretched and insecure bridge, the first we had seen in the country, and constructed of branches of trees, covered with a thick layer of clay; and on reaching a village at a short distance from the spot, all our carriers, as if by instinct, simultaneously dropped their burdens, and scampered off as fast as if they had been running for their lives. In a few moments we were surrounded by great numbers of the male inhabitants of the place, who were armed with bows and arrows; and, pretending not to understand a word of the Houssa language, the fellows snatched up the deserted property, and before we had time to prevent them, or ask what they intended doing, went off with it at an inconceivable rate, we following on horseback, till tired and out of breath, the blacks halted at another assemblage of huts on the banks of the same stream we had crossed the preceding day, forming a portion of Tabria. Resting there for a short period, the good-natured people voluntarily caught up the baggage a second time, and passing with all haste over a bridge to the opposite side of the river, finally stopped in front of the house of one of the head men of the place.

The village forms the remaining part of the before mentioned town, with which it is connected by a miserable old bridge, and it contains a great population.

Coming at length to an explanation with the martial carriers of our baggage, we had it lodged in a large empty hut for the night; but the fellows returned to their town very much dissatisfied with the trifle with which they were remunerated; for they had hoped that on entering Tabria the property would have become their own.

Tabria consists of two towns, lying on the margins of a stream or river called the Mayyarrow, which are connected together by a wooden bridge; and both places may contain eighteen thousand inhabitants. They are occasionally visited by the sovereigns of Nyffé.

An exterminating civil war had been raging in the kingdom, and was still in active operation at the period of our arrival; one party of the natives siding with Edrisi, a pagan, the rightful heir to the throne of his deceased father; and the other leaning on the side of Mohammed, a Mussulman, who had disputed his brother's right of succession. By far the major part of the people, being pagans, were decidedly in favour of the former prince; but the other having invited the Falatahs to his assistance, had completely beaten his less fortunate brother, and it was generally expected that in the next campaign Edrisi would be driven from the country; or, if taken prisoner, decapitated without mercy. A cessation of hostilities had been resolved on by the belligerent parties on the day we entered Tabria; but the contest would be resumed, it was affirmed, after the rains.

The queen dowager of Nyffé, a decrepit and infirm old lady, one of whose eyes had been accidentally shot out of her head by an arrow, resided at Tabria, with the head wife of Mohammed. That prince himself was at a place three days' journey from the town; and the old queen having intimated to Captain Clapperton, that it would be well for him to visit her son, before he quitted the country, with a suitable present, my master thought proper to accede to the wishes of the queen mother; and leaving me in charge of the baggage, &c. carried his intention into effect on the 21st of April.

During the Captain's absence I used daily to take a ramble on the borders of the May-Yarrow, and amuse myself with my gun, plenty of game existing in the vicinity. The river is serpentine, and of irregular breadth; in some places so narrow that a person may easily jump across, and at others widening from twenty to thirty yards; its depth generally fluctuating between eight and twelve feet. Thousands of monkeys inhabit the leafy branches of the trees that overhang the stream; and play all manner of mischievous tricks on the people who may venture to stroll in that direction. Going one day with the design of shooting guinea-fowl, I unintentionally killed two of these little animals, and wounded a third, which fell, apparently dead, at my feet. I took them to our lodgings, and the hostess immediately offered forty cowries for each of them; but, perceiving signs of life in the wounded monkey, I kept it, with the intention of ascertaining whether it would recover, and spared her the slain ones. The good woman, having skinned and broiled the animals, sat down to partake of them with two or three of her neighbours, and after making a sumptuous repast, declared the flesh to be sweeter and richer than that of any animal with which she was acquainted. One of our landlady's guests, falling in love with the living monkey, took the liberty of stealing it in the night, when, no doubt, it shared the fate of its companions.

On the 24th the usurper's eldest daughter paid me a visit, bringing with her a present of yams and rice; and being a very agreeable girl, I solicited her so pressingly to take tea with me, that the princess accepted the invitation, after which we took a walk together through the town, arm in arm, *à l'Europe.* The inhabitants of Fabria stood staring at us with open mouths, for some seconds, and wondering greatly what could be the meaning of so singular a custom, when they set up so astounding a roar of laughter, as put her royal highness fairly out of countenance; and I was obliged to re-conduct her to our lodgings with the utmost haste. On entering them, I made her a trifling present, with which she was infinitely pleased; and the princess of the powerful kingdom of

Nyffé went away dancing, singing, and capering, and promised to honour me with another visit on the morning of the next day.

The Falatahs left Coulfo for Soccasoo the day after our arrival at Tabria, with a thousand slaves, some of whom were partizans of Edrisi, who had been taken prisoners by that prince. Besides this, they compelled Mohammed to present them with four hundred tobes, which with the slaves they took to Sultan Bello, as a partial recompence for the services they had rendered his cause in the late desolating campaign. Mohammed, called by his people the *Magee*, was a most cruel and inhuman prince, and the greatest scourge that had ever afflicted his country. He had poisoned, it was confidently reported, a younger brother and two of his sons, for having ventured to express their opinion against his wild and inordinate ambition, in attempting to rule the kingdom against the interests and inclinations of the people; and because they, in common with their countrymen, hated the Falatahs most cordially, for the willingness and alacrity they had ever displayed to embroil Nyffé in civil war, to the advancement of their own influence, and the aggrandizement of their own power.

The war was still raging in Nyffé on my return to that country from Houssa, with far different prospects. The pagan brother, Edrisi, had recovered from the effects of his defeats, and gained important advantages over Mohammed and the Falatahs, his allies. This good success was owing to a large body of men having come to Edrisi's assistance from Benin, and inspired with fresh courage his disspirited followers. These individuals had proceeded up the Quorra in canoes, and landed at *Mulagee*, a small town in Nyffé situated on the banks of that river; a junction was then immediately formed with the pagan natives of the country, and an attack made on the Mussulmans with European muskets, a great number of which they had brought with them; when the latter, with the Magee at their head, were defeated with dreadful slaughter, and the Falatahs being the objects against whom the fire-arms of the people of Benin were more particularly directed, very few of them, comparatively speaking, escaped with life. The week before I revisited Tabria, Mohammed had experienced another signal overthrow, and it was generally believed by the inhabitants that the remnant of the Falatahs, who had been so roughly handled, would be obliged to abandon Nyffé in a few days, and return, discomfited, to Soccasoo, in which case Edrisi would reign in the kingdom, and Mohammed either follow the Falatahs, or lose his life by remaining behind.

On the 25th Captain Clapperton returned from the camp of Mohammed, and on Tuesday the 2nd of May we proceeded on our journey by a path winding along the delightful banks of the May-yarrow. Passing near to Gonda, a walled village, and crossing a broad but shallow stream, we entered by one of the gates into the town of Coulfo, which is distant from Tabria, in a direct line, only four miles.

Coulfo is the most considerable market town in Nyffé, and the general emporium of that part of Africa. It contains between fifteen and sixteen thousand *resident* inhabitants, and, like most towns of any consideration or extent in the country, is surrounded by a high wall, outside of which is a deep and broad ditch.

The May-yarrow flows by the wall of the town, and is a source of much comfort to the inhabitants, particularly by reason of its imparting an agreeable coolness to the atmosphere, which is very desirable in the heat of the day. Markets are daily held at Coulfo, and an immense variety of articles, of native and foreign manufacture, are exposed for sale in them. Traders resort in vast numbers from Bornou and Soccasoo to the north and east, and from the sea coast to the west, with the produce and manufactures of their respective countries, for which they find ready buyers in the town. Slaves, horses, asses, and horned cattle, are brought from every part of Africa, as well as silk, wrought and unwrought, cotton, natron, beads, turbans, scarlet caps, goora nuts, malaguetta pepper, red wood, &c.; the traffic in which is carried on to an indefinite extent.

The inhabitants of Coulfo, like the natives of many parts of the ivory and gold coasts, anoint their bodies with softened clay, or pounded wood of the same colour, with which a little grease is invariably mixed. They are principally Mahommedans, and perform a few of the rites and ceremonies prescribed by the prophet, such as praying a given number of times in the day, frequent lustrations of the hands and face, and a rigid adherence to the fast of the Rhamadan. In other respects, however, they do not conform to the moral precepts of the Koran, drunkenness being their ruling passion; and so addicted are they to falsehood and deception, and so generally prevalent are these vices become, that all sense of their impropriety is lost amongst the people, and it is not considered discreditable for the most respectable individuals in the town to practise these arts upon each other. Theft also may be said to be encouraged, in some degree; for, like the ancient Spartans, parents praise the spirit and ingenuity of the junior branches of the community who pilfer articles of trifling value from their neighbours, without being detected in the act.

The females set off their charms to the best

advantage, by staining their hair, teeth, hands, and feet, in a similar manner to that of the widow Zuma, which has already been described. This practice, which is common to all ranks, and without adhering to which beauty cannot exist in their eyes, in all probability is derived from the Moors or Saracens, many of whose habits were copied by the natives at the time of their irruption into the country, and still maintain the ascendancy which they at first assumed. The more glaring the colour of the dye on the persons of the *fair* sex, the more fascinating is the object in the eyes of the men of Coulfo—hence the pains every young woman takes to attract the admiration and win the love of her male companion by bright blue hair, red teeth, yellow hands, &c.; but above all, by keeping her body supple and yielding by the use of red clay. It is hardly possible to conceive the jealousies, and the thousand other afflicting passions that spring up in the breast of a lady, if the person of another excels her own in brilliancy of colouring. I have seen the poor things shed floods of tears on this account; and on one occasion, in particular, was greatly moved at observing a girl of our landlady's acquaintance sighing and sobbing in a corner of our room, because *Nuggree*, her lover, had told her a few minutes before, that her teeth were not quite of so bright a red as those of her female companion!

Whilst we remained at Coulfo, a messenger from our friend, the king of Boussa, arrived with a present of a beautiful little mare for my master, accompanied by a female slave, who brought butter and rice from the Queen to Captain Clapperton and myself. His majesty had desired the man to caution us against partaking of any food that might be sent from the female relatives of the usurper of Nyffé, it being their avowed intention to poison us by that means. This information, joined with other circumstances, rendered us infinitely more suspicious than we had previously been, and obliged us to use greater caution in accepting presents of provisions from doubtful quarters. From that time it was our usual custom to interrogate the individual bringing butter, &c. and if he evinced the least reluctance to answer our questions, or betrayed the slightest symptoms of fear or timidity in our presence, he was compelled to eat part of the suspected articles himself, and in case of refusal, dismissed with a severe whipping, and his presents thrown away. We found this plan extremely serviceable to us, if we might be allowed to judge from the hasty retreat of more than one of these good-natured individuals.

The new moon, to catch a glimpse of which every eye in Coulfo was on the stretch, was seen on Tuesday the 8th of May, and her first appearance welcomed by a flourish of trumpets from the inhabitants.* This concluded the fast of the Rhamadan; and the following day was kept as a holiday for feasting and rejoicing by every individual in the place, amogsnt all classes, and of every sect and party,—thousands of both sexes from the neighbouring towns and villages flocking into it, in order to partici-

---

* A ceremony very similar to that which was formerly in use among the Jews, as may be seen by perusing the third verse of the 31st Psalm :—" Blow up the trumpet in the new moon, in the time appointed, on our solemn feast-day."

pate in the festivities and amusements of the occasion. Men and boys, old women and young maidens, slave and free, Mahommedan and Pagan, forgot all distinctions of rank, and difference in age and modes of worship,—and joining in the song and the dance, drank palm-wine and *booza* together, and before the morning was well over, all hands became comfortably drunk. Groups of persons might be seen in the afternoon, rambling from one end of the town to the other, dancing, capering, tumbling, and hallooing, some reeling to and fro, scarcely able to stand, others insensible from excessive intoxication; some flung into the river by their boisterous companions, and dragged out again half drowned; some smiting their breasts, and calling upon the name of the Prophet; others hurrying about in every direction; fighting, praying, laughing, weeping; but all, from the governor and his ladies to the meanest bondmen and slaves,—all drunk in a greater or less degree.

It was now inexpressibly—insufferably hot; not a single zephyr panted upon the motionless trees, and the intensity of the sun's rays threatened to set fire to the tenantless huts of the inhabitants. About five or six o'clock a sultry haze obscured the firmament, which dispersing some time afterwards, a solemn, fearful calm succeeded, and continued for an hour or two, the people still enjoying their noisy revelry, and loud bursts of merriment resounding from every quarter of the town. We, apprehensive of what was to come after, kept our eyes intently fixed on the eastern horizon, and at length espied a small dark cloud slowly rising from that quarter of the heavens. Immediately after the appearance of this object, faint flashes of lightning, and distant peals of thunder following in rapid succession, convinced us that a tornado was approaching. The people at last understanding these symptoms, all was hurry, bustle, and confusion, in a moment—the music and dancing suddenly ceased—the drunken became sober—a deep, wild, thrilling cry was raised by the women, and answered by screams of affright from the children and young persons. Meanwhile, the peals of thunder became infinitely louder and more appalling, and the lightning more intensely vivid than before: the clouds in the east gradually rolling towards the zenith in denser and heavier masses, a large portion of the heavens was presently clothed in almost midnight darkness, when the western horizon suddenly opened, and a sea of liquid fire streaming from that direction, added a sterner and yet more dreadful grandeur to the firmament, exposing by its yellowish glare all the horrors and blackness of the scene. The sable curtain that overhung our heads, was rent asunder shortly after with a frightful explosion, causing the earth to tremble and shake as if the Almighty had set his foot upon the world, and reproached the people for their wickedness; while the shuddering war-cry, and the tumult and wailings of the multitude, mingling with the hollow blast of the tempest, produced on us an indescribable effect, and awoke in me an exalted, but painful and tremulous emotion of soul, that had nearly overpowered me.

To increase the consternation that was depicted on every countenance, the town of *Bali*, containing eleven hundred houses, and situated about half a mile from Coulfo, was set on fire by the lightning; and the piercing cries of its terrified inhabitants floating dismally into the latter town, were re-echoed by thousands of human voices, which produced a concert of melancholy sounds, that caused even the domestic animals to shrink with fear.

The hurricane and rain at length ceased, the noise of the people was hushed into silence, and the tempestuous elements sank from horrid sublimity into their previous state of awful repose. I have witnessed many tornados in other parts of the globe;

> "But never till that night, never till then,
> Did I go through a tempest dropping fire."

Next morning I took a walk through the town, and in the country in its vicinity: the air, as it generally is after such visitations, was delightfully fresh and pleasant, but the earth was covered with afflicting proofs of the tremendous power of the storm; superb trees, through the trunks of which, if scooped out, a coach might easily pass, were torn up by the roots, and their gigantic branches shivered into splinters; whilst others were indeed standing, but scathed and blackened from the effects of the lightning, and entirely stripped of their verdant foliage. Fragments and roofs of huts, many of them yet smouldering, were scattered in every direction; and here and there the dead body of a bird or beast, which had perished the preceding night, might be met with.

The destitute inhabitants of Bali came to Coulfo, the day after their town had been reduced to ashes, to tell their simple tale of distress, and solicit the assistance of their more favoured neighbours. I was pleased to see their story listened to with tears, and their sorrowful condition ameliorated, with a benevolence and zeal that effectually covered the bad qualities of the people of Coulfo, and made one forget for a moment that they possessed any. In a conversation with one of the sufferers in the ill-fated town, I learned that several mothers had perished in the flames, while in the act of escaping from them with their tender offspring slung to their backs; and it was supposed that many of the male sex had shared in the like calamity, as they were missing, and no intelligence whatever had transpired respecting them. One individual, bowed down with years, had snatched up in his arms a little boy who was crossing his path, screaming with terror; but, just as he had reached the outskirts of the burning town, and was congratulating himself on his good fortune, in having preserved his own and the child's life so unexpectedly, a moving mass of fire, whirled by the wind, suddenly fell upon him, and both he and his charge were scorched to death, in sight of their sorrowing relatives.

The town of Bali soon rose from its ruins, and the people, by their merriment and vivacity, seemed to forget, a month or two afterwards, that any such calamity had befallen it.

The country for miles round Coulfo is studded with walled towns, open villages, and clusters of houses; and so jealous are the inhabitants of one of these places of the superiority, imaginary or real, whether as regards personal bravery or success in slave-catching, of another, that, like the natives of rival parishes in Cornwall, before the introduction of Methodism into that county, or the different sects and orders which agitate Ireland at the present time, formally challenge each other, and meet by appointment to try the prowess and superiority of their respective parties. On such occasions, the combatants arm themselves with bludgeons, bows and arrows, and spears; and the conflict is, in almost every instance, prosecuted with the bitterness and animosity of the most ruthless savages, frequently terminating in the death or capture of numbers of each party, when the latter are uniformly sold into slavery. Just at the period of our arrival at Coulfo, the inhabitants of the walled town of Koofoo, situated but a short distance from the former place, having captured and sold, contrary to custom, the wife of a man belonging to a neighbouring village, who was supposed to have been slain in one of these engagements, a mutual system of retaliation and petty warfare was the consequence, which had embroiled all the country in domestic dissensions; and their war-cry, of all sounds, next to their death-yell, the most truly terrific, could be distinctly heard at our lodgings in

Coulfo every evening. A person connected with either of the disturbed towns could not venture out alone, or unarmed, without exposing himself to be shot at or pierced by his inveterate antagonists, who made it a constant practice to prowl about the country, and spring, tiger-like, upon any unsuspecting victim whom pleasure or business had induced to quit the boundaries of his native village. These intestine commotions, united to the formidable civil war that was desolating the kingdom of Nyffé, had caused the minds of the people to be in a perpetual state of fermentation and alarm, occasioning their angry and incited passions to have the ascendancy over their milder virtues; and to this cause is attributable, more than to any other, the absence of that kindness and hospitality, amongst the natives generally, which were so cheerfully bestowed upon us in the less civilized kingdoms of Yariba and Borghoo,—although even the people of Nyffé were by no means destitute of the gentle charities of life.

The severe and continued indisposition that both my master and myself experienced, obliged us to remain in the city of Coulfo six or seven weeks; but, getting better at the termination of that period, we departed on the nineteenth of June, and passing through Koofoo, where we slept, and several other villages, encamped outside the walled town of Bullabulla on the 21st of the same month. At that place I was attacked with dysentery, a truly frightful disorder, that causes hope to die within the patient, and puts him altogether out of the love of life. The pain it occasioned me was so great, and its effects so distressing, that I was unable to keep a regular journal of occurrences until my arrival at Kano. On the road to that city my sufferings were too acute to be described; and it was not unusual for me to lag behind the rest of the party, and, dismounting from my horse, to roll myself in the dust, in the hope of relieving the agony of the moment, where I remained panting on the naked earth, till my master, alarmed at my long absence, would light large fires, by the smoke of which I was directed to his resting-place. On entering the tent, it was my custom, without uttering a word, to fling myself on a

196   AUTHOR'S ILLNESS.

mat, and, embracing my pillow,* to sleep, or rather *endeavour* to sleep till morning. By this means I acquired a habit of groaning in my slumbers, of which I could not completely divest myself, even for some months after my return to England. Whenever we came to a stream which was too deep to ford, and unfurnished with a ferry-boat, being too weak myself to swim, my generous master used to take me on his shoulders, and, oftentimes at the imminent risk of his own life, carry me in safety to the opposite bank.

We journeyed over a wooded and partially cultivated country, through several populous walled towns and open villages, and arrived at Guâri, in Kashna, on Monday the 3d of July.

Leaving that place on the following Friday we continued our course, and entered the

* Captain Clapperton and myself procured, whilst in the interior, two large pillows, covered with leather, and stuffed full of hair, which we found extremely serviceable to us, in consequence of the grateful coolness thus imparted during the warm nights of the dry season. Instead of laying our heads on the pillow, we used to clasp it in our arms, and, when saturated with perspiration, it was thrown aside, till becoming dry it was again embraced.

western gate of Zaria, a considerable Falatah town, and the capital of the province of Zeg Zeg, on Monday the 10th.

The country to the eastward of the town was unspeakably fine, and almost clear of wood; and looked as fresh and beautiful as the richest parts of England in the summer months. Plantations of rice and cotton; fields of undulating corn; meadows covered with a lovely verdure; and gentle slopes with herds and flocks grazing and browzing on them, looked as picturesque and rural as any landscape I had beheld in my own, or indeed any other country.

We remained at Zaria a week, when we again set out; and traversing a country charmingly diversified by hills and dales, streamlets of water, groves of superb trees peopled with birds of the gayest plumage, and enclosures of Indian corn, yams, indigo, the cotton plant, wheat, millet, &c. we arrived at Kano on Thursday the 20th of July.

CHAPTER VII.

Residence at Kano—Captain Clapperton leaves for Soccasoo—History of Pasko, the Houssa Interpreter—Pasko's robberies and confinement—Return of the Captain with the Godado, after an ineffectual attempt to reach Soccatoo—His second departure from Kano—His Letters.

WE were mortified beyond measure to learn of Hat Sallah, my master's agent on the former journey, that the Bornouese and Falatahs were at war, and in consequence thereof that all communication between the two kingdoms had been effectually cut off. On hearing of our arrival, the countenances of the Arabs in the city brightened up; for they fancied that we should be the means of bringing about a permanent peace between the belligerents, the war having occasioned the ruin of several of them, and threatened the prosperity of the whole.

I had received instructions from Captain Clapperton to remain in Kano with the baggage, whilst he undertook a journey to Soccasoo and back, it being unnecessary to have the goods conveyed so far out of the road to Bornou. Therefore on Thursday the 24th of July, every arrangement having been previously made, my master came to bid me adieu, and give me final instructions relative to proceeding to Bornou and Tripoli, in case of his death, or of any unforeseen accident that might befall him. On this occasion each of us was much moved, and we parted with that unaffected sorrow which the circumstances in which we were placed were so eminently calculated to call forth. Our little party had left their native country full of hope and enterprising spirit, and we had seen them sicken and die by our sides without being in a condition to migitate their sufferings, or " smooth down their lonely pillow." Like the characters in Mozart's " Farewell," they had dropped one by one; and they were buried in a strange land, far from the graves of their fathers, with scarce a memento to point out the solitary spot. These were my thoughts at the moment of separation from my valued master, whom I may justly style the preserver of my life. I knew that it was by no means unlikely we might never meet again, and we were well assured, that in the event of our dissolutions when apart, no one could be found to close our eyes, still less to perform the rites of Christian burial over our remains. My master therefore left me with emotion. For my own part, I was yet, if possible, more sensibly agitated; I was ill with dysentery at the time, *very* ill; and throwing myself on my couch as soon as the Captain was out of sight, I did not arise from it again for twenty-four hours.

Kano is one of the most important and considerable cities in Soudan, and is a general mart for all sorts of merchandize. The indigo, manufactured by the inhabitants, has the reputation of producing a richer and more permanent dye than is to be met with in any other part of Africa whatever, and is on this account in very high estimation with all classes of people. The population of the town, on a rough computation, probably exceeds forty thousand souls, the major part of whom are slaves, but treated with kindness and forbearance by their masters. Arabs and Moors resort thither from the Barbary States, for the purposes of trade, and their goods realise an immense profit in the market, remunerating them with a rapid fortune. The wall of the city, thirty feet in height, and of proportionable thickness, encompasses a space of nearly ten English miles; but upwards of two-thirds of the ground enclosed is taken up with morasses, plantations, and gardens, the dwelling of the inhabitants occupying the remaining portion. The houses are built in a square form, after the Moorish fashion, of flat roofs covered with hardened clay interlaced with palm leaves; and are on the whole roomy and comfortable abodes.

The air of Kano is close and insalubrious, and rendered yet more unwholesome, in consequence of the number of stagnant pools of water, partly filled with putrifying animal and vegetable substances, which are tolerated in the town. A most disagreeable odour is exhaled by this means; while a large morass intersecting the city from east to west, into which the filth of the inhabitants is indiscriminately emptied, tends still further towards its general unhealthiness. The dead bodies of slaves are frequently cast into this morass, exposed to the action of the air or visits of birds of prey; and it is truly shocking to observe their mangled members in a state of decomposition, and their fleshless bones bleaching in the sun in the very heart of the town.

This painful and disgusting spectacle I was oftentimes obliged to be a witness to, a week rarely passing without one or more of these unregretted corpses being flung into the common receptacle, and left to the gaze of the people, amongst whom all sense of delicacy in this respect seemed to have been stifled by gross familiarity with this revolting custom; by reason of this the inhabitants pass by the decaying bodies of their fellow creatures with no greater symptoms of repugnance than if they had been the remains of their own domestic animals.

I had scarcely been in Kano a fortnight, when Pasko, our Houssa interpreter, absconded with a few articles of trifling value, and after a diligent and persevering search of three days, he was found concealed under a heap of yams, in the house of the mother to a female he had recently married. He was accompanied to our house by his better half, sobbing all the way, who begged me, with much earnestness, to forgive her husband for the offence he had been guilty of, which I consented to do, but not till after he had received a severe scolding, and promised never again to perpetrate a crime of a similar nature against me or any one else.

As this old man's history may not be altogether uninteresting, inasmuch as it shows, in a lively point of view, the ridiculous superstitions of his countrymen, imbibed in their infant years, which no circumstance or change of scene in their after life can wholly eradicate, I hope I may be excused for giving a short account of his adventures previously to his being engaged in the African mission, as repeated solemnly to me several times from his own lips, and after that period till his arrival with us at Kano, drawn from personal observation.

Pasko's native name was *Abbu Becr*, and although this is without doubt a Mohammedan appellation, he knew nothing more of Islamism than its name, being in reality a Pagan. He was born in the district of Goober, and was brother to the reigning prince of that country, who at the period of the subjugation of the neighbouring provinces to the yoke of Danfodio, Bello's father, ridiculed that wily conqueror's pretensions to sanctity, and rose with his people to dispute his further advances into Houssa. In an engagement with the Falatahs, in which Pasko distinguished himself, his brother was suddenly metamorphosed into a white elephant! and as soon as he was conscious of his melancholy change, rushed into the thickest of the fight, trampling to death upwards of two hundred of his adversaries, who were panic-struck at the unexpected appearance of so formidable an animal amongst them; but rallying a short time afterwards, they winged their arrows so effectually, that the body of the enormous beast became like that of a porcupine, being literally covered with them; and this fact, joined to his extraordinary exertions and loss of blood, made the intrepid elephant quit the field of battle. Lifting up Pasko, therefore, from the ground with his proboscis, he repaired to a neighbouring forest, and dropping his charge, was transfixed, like Lot's wife to the spot, by the same invisible power that had been so instrumental in bringing about his previous alteration of form and nature. Here he stood, without the power of stirring an inch, or of moving a limb, and although Pasko's bitter lamentations were heard at a considerable distance, the inexorable deity was deaf to these violent bursts of sorrow; but his fraternal tenderness would not suffer Pasko to leave the place till he had the felicity of beholding trees and shrubs grow round the body of the petrified elephant; which third miracle took place about three hours after the former ones, and completely hid the transformed from the most prying curiosity!

The remainder of Pasko's history is entitled to a greater share of credence. A year or two subsequent to the above singular occurrence, as Pasko was dancing by the light of the moon, with several of his companions, he was kidnapped by a marauding party of Falatahs, and sold to a Gonja trader. This man not treating him with the kindness he expected, to be revenged Pasko took the liberty of robbing him of all his goods, and decamping in the night; he was, however, apprehended the next evening, in a state of intoxication, dancing with a dozen females, and taken back to his master, who re-sold him to a native of Ashantee. By this master he was taken considerable notice of, and sent, along with many others, to his own country (Ashantee); but no great while after his arrival thither he committed a second serious misdemeanour, for which offence he was driven to the sea-side, and sold to the master of a Portuguese schooner, then lying at Whydah. On her voyage to Bahia, the vessel was captured by an English sloop of war, and Pasko was liberated; but consented to remain with the British, and serve as an ordinary seaman. He was, however, taken from his employment by Mr.

Belzoni, in order to accompany him in his attempt to reach Tombuctoo by way of Fez; but that enterprizing traveller dying of dysentery, Pasko returned to his duties in the British navy, where he remained till engaged by Captain Clapperton, in the joint capacity of servant to Captain Pearce, and general interpreter to the mission.

Pasko was no more than five feet in height, with hands and arms disproportionately long: his face was open and expressive, if a mouth extending literally from ear to ear can impart an enviable cast of feature to the human countenance; and his cheek was furrowed with the tatto mark of the Houssa nation (eight deep scars, inflicted by a rude instrument during boyhood). His nose was excessively broad and flat, and his lips resembled, as nearly as possible, the famous German sausage ornamented; and these were, with large teeth, of pearly whiteness, which were generally exposed by a perpetual grin playing upon his countenance. But there was an undefinable expression of low cunning in his dark, wandering eye, and an habitual restlessness in his manner which induced one to suspect that there was more of evil in him than he was willing should be detected, and which he strove to disguise under forced stupidity and carelessness which in reality did not belong to his disposition. It is somewhat odd that Pasko, plain as his appearance most undoubtedly was, should have entertained the strange notion that almost every female who saw him, of whatever hue, nation, or religion she might be, could not help falling in love with him at first sight, imagining that his intellectual physiognomy possessed some peculiar attraction—an oil of rhodium,—which fascinated all beholders. Hence, secure of the affections of the softer sex, his behaviour to them was not always graced by that studied civility, and agreeableness of manner, which are the characteristics of most gallants; what others were obliged to entreat and sigh for as a favour, Pasko demanded as a right, and enforced his pretensions with an eloquence so commanding, that according to his own asseverations at least, his advances were never repelled by coldness or disdain. At the period of his engaging himself with the African mission, he might have been about sixty years of age, but looked considerably older; and the above unaccountable feeling of his had lost none of its intensity at so advanced a period of life. Like Aaron's rod, it swallowed up every other passion; and as will be seen by the numerous wives with whom he was accommodated, and the scrapes he fell into by their means, Pasko subscribed, with all his heart, to the anathema of the Poet:

"Curse on all laws save those which *Love* has made!"

At Badagry, one of the wives of Adólee, the king, fell desperately in love with the self-enamoured Pasko, and strove to awaken his sensibility by a present of a bottle of rum; but the latter being observed sneaking near the king's house at unseasonable hours, was threatened with death if he attempted to display his alluring accomplishments before the illustrious female inmates, to the infinite uneasiness of his majesty's mind. Pasko, with whom foolhardiness was in no very high esteem, went off in great dudgeon, and never repeated his visit to the seraglio, confining himself within doors as much as possible. This seclusion, however, could not screen him from the resentment of the slighted lady, for as he was standing outside our house one day, a stone, flung with great force from her own *fair* hand, struck Pasko so violent a blow on the breast, that it completely ejected every spark of tenderness he might have entertained for her, and he vowed to embrace the earliest opportunity of being revenged. At Jannah he forgot his disappointment in the endearing expressions lavished upon his extraordinary beauty by a girl of that place, whom he married agreeably to the custom of the country, and took with him to Katunga, in Yariba. The attachment seemed to be reciprocal for some time; and Pasko was so bound up in the blandishments of his spouse, that he was loth to expose her delicate person to the dangers of a journey to Bornou, and proposed remaining in that city, instead of continuing in the service of the mission; his better half relishing the proposal extremely well, and seconding it with all the weight of her influence. Aspiring, however, to the society of the wives of his majesty of Katunga, and those of his great men, Pasko's rib fell into the temptation of tippling and carousing with them at all seasons, and indulged in this disgraceful propensity to so great an excess, that she rarely returned to the arms of her impatient husband in a sober state; and was, moreover, frequently seen in the company of younger men than he. All this at length reaching the ears of Captain Clapperton, she was dismissed his service, but retaken at the piteous lamentations and entreaties of Pasko, who declared, blubbering all the while, that he could not survive her loss, so strongly was she linked to him by the silken bands of love! The amiable lady, nevertheless, the morning before our departure from Katunga, rising from the couch of her unsuspecting companion, decamped with the coral beads and other trinkets he had received of Mrs. Belzoni whilst in England, and was never seen or heard of after. Pasko consoled himself with the reflection that the woman was certainly deranged, or she never could have treated a person of his consideration so unhandsomely!

At Wow Wow he buried all his griefs and vexations in the embraces of a fresh wife he had received of the generous Zuma; but it being unlawful to accept such a present without having first obtained the consent of the king, Mohammed compelled him to return the dear object of his affections, much against his own inclination, and the unfortunate lover determined not to marry again in a hurry. A young woman in Kano however overturned his resolution, and he left me in the manner which has already been related. Pasko never troubled his head much about religous matters, adopting the prevailing opinions about them in the various countries through which he might happen to pass: thus, he was a Christian in England, a Pagan in Yariba and Borghoo, and a Mohammedan in the Falatah empire; although the superstitious notions of his childhood clung like instinct to his manhood and declining years, evidently disposing him to lean towards Paganism, as the best and most convenient doctrine with which he was acquainted.

My master unexpectedly returned to Kano

in September, accompanied by the Godado (prime minister of sultan Bello) and several Falatahs of less consequence, the road to Soccasoo having been found impassable by reason of the rain that had fallen. After remaining with me three or four days, Captain Clapperton left the city a second time, and entered the capital of Houssa in safety, on Thursday the 19th of October.

On the night of the 1st of November Pasko eloped with his Kano wife, taking with him six pairs of scissors and a pistol. On missing him next morning, I made an inquiry after him in the city, but no one could give me the least account of the fugitive, till a person informed me of his having met him with a woman at an early hour on the road to Zeg Zeg. As soon as this information was comunicated to me, I secured the baggage in an apartment of our house, and took the key to Hat Sallah, with a request that he would suffer no one to enter it till my return. Although I was by no means recovered from the painful illness which had for so long a time afflicted me, I immediately mounted my horse, and desiring Abdalfitha, one of our Arab servants to accompany me on another, took the road to Quorra, a large town in Zeg Zeg, and travelled with unusual speed. A journey of four days brought us to Roma, on entering which town we were told that Pasko had just before quitted it; but our horses being almost knocked up, we could proceed no further on that day, by reason whereof we were obliged to remain there till the following morning.

We had not been in the place, however, more than an hour, when some of the inhabitants came with the news that they had seen Pasko in a woman's house near the market-place; and as soon as I had ascertained that this was actually the case, I hired a dozen stout men to watch at the gates, and apprehend him if he attempted to escape from the town. Meanwhile, being exhausted myself with the violent exercise I had been necessitated to take, I ordered Abdulfitha to proceed to the place of his concealment, and endeavour to secure the criminal, which he succeeded in doing without even the shadow of opposition on Pasko's part, and presently after brought him to me. The old fellow, with the most unconcerned air imaginable, wondered I had taken so much pains on his account, affirming that he had taken a jaunt into the country for a day or two, in order to amuse himself by shooting a few pigeons for my use, for he felt for me in my long indisposition! and that it was his intention to return to Kano as soon as he had accomplished his charitable purpose. His wife, not liking this species of enjoyment, had left him the preceding day, and had gone back to her mother's house. Pasko, having made this ingenious defence, I gave him a severe lecture for having left Kano without my knowledge or consent; but as he showed symptoms of contrition, and promising solemnly to behave with more circumspection for the future, I cheerfully forgave him; and we retired to rest.

On our return we halted at a small village about twelve miles from Kano, where we slept. In the night, Pasko, watching a favorable opportunity, stole unobserved out of the hut with all my money, which I had concealed, for its better security, in my stocking, together with my guns, pistols, and in fact every thing belonging to me, with the exception of the horse. The manner in which the robbery was discovered was as follows:—About two o'clock in the morning, being thirsty, I called on Pasko several times to fetch me a little water, but receiving no answer, I arose, and approaching the mat on which he had lain down the preceding evening, caught hold of what I conceived to be his head, and shook it violently. Still receiving no answer, I became alarmed, and instantly striking a light, I found, not Pasko's corpse stretched on the mat as I expected, but a slaughtered sheep! which had been sent me from the chief of the town, in its stead, and which the artful old scoundrel had placed in that position, enveloping the head of the animal in one of my woollen caps, for the purpose of deceiving me! as Abdulfitha had been in the habit of laying his hand on Pasko's head at intervals during the night, in order to ascertain that all was right. The thief had stripped me almost naked; but wrapping a blanket round my person, I rode hastily with

Abdulfitha, by star-light, to Kano, and arrived there early in the morning. As soon as Hat Sallah had arisen, I simply told him how I had been served, when he immediately sent several individuals in quest of the robber, who returned with him two days after. This was enjoyment with a vengeance; so being determined he should take no more rural excursions, I ordered the prisoner to be heavily ironed, and confined in the common dungeon till the return of the governor of Kano from a town called Fanisoe: this took place two or three days only before my departure, and on the same day Pasko being examined by his excellency, and having taken an oath in his presence that he would not again desert me till the arrival of Captain Clapperton from Soccasoo, he was set at large in the city.

I saw a slave in Kano whose fore teeth were cut and pointed, a custom I thought peculiar to the coast, and some of the islands in the South Seas. The man's appearance was most ferocious; and so sullen and reserved was he, that he refused to answer any interrogations that were put to him, although I was inclined to believe that he had perpetrated some flagrant crime, as he was so far on his way to Badagry, whither he would not have been sent, if his character were not of the very worst description.

One day, as I was walking to the governor's house, I espied a white man at some distance; I ran after him as fast as my strength would permit me, and thought at first he was an apparition; but on approaching within a few yards, and the man suddenly stopping, I immediately perceived that he was a leper. His head, neck, and shoulders were bared, and the skin, covered with a thick scurf, had a ghastly and cadaverous appearance. When he turned to look at me, I could not forbear shuddering, and felt so peculiar a sensation creep through my frame, that I willingly laid hold of a date tree growing near the spot, in order to keep myself in an erect position. The wool, nose, and lips, were entirely negro, and when these were contrasted with his pale, diseased skin, the leper scarcely maintained the appearance of a human being. We had seen a woman in Katunga afflicted with a similar loathsome malady; but its effects in the latter instance were not nearly so visibly disgusting. Both the unhappy individuals were vagrants, and shunned, like the lazars of Italy, by their fellow-creatures. Their life must, indeed, have been a burden to them; for the disease, preying upon their vitals, threatened to terminate their wretched career very speedily; and to add to their sorrows, they had no where to lay their heads.

I had purchased a young ostrich of a Tuarick, who had brought it from the desert, shortly after our arrival at Kano, and the animal soon became so tame, that it would follow me like a dog. In two months after I had it in my possession it grew amazingly, and I was in hopes of bringing it to England with me; but an envious Arab in the city, whose inveterate dislike to every thing belonging to the Christians he took no pains to conceal, cut off its head, and artfully attributed it to accident. Meeting the fellow in the street a short time afterwards, I belaboured his sides so effectually with a stout stick which I held in my hand, that he ran off bellowing with a complaint to the governor, who, after listening patiently to his story, observed, with a very significant look, that he was quite sure the drubbing he had received must have been inflicted *by accident,* and dismissed the malicious Arab without granting the redress he sought.

A wealthy Nyffé man had in his possession, in Kano, two individuals, male and female, so excessively small, that although they were nearly thirty years of age, their height did not exceed forty inches. Each of them had been brought from a place called Goorma, and they had left their native country at a very early period of life; insomuch, that they had no recollection of their parents, or of any thing connected with the manners and customs of their countrymen. None but particular friends of the proprietor were allowed to see these human beings in miniature, and even they were introduced only at particular seasons. For my part, I often visited them, and their innocent playful manners greatly diverted me. They were extremely chatty and good-tempered, and their agility was as remarkable as their size was diminutive. I offered to purchase them; but not altogether admiring my white skin, they refused to quit the hospitable roof of their owner, who candidly acknowledged that he was so much attached to the dwarfs, that he had resolved never to force their inclinations to a measure they disliked in their hearts.

When I was able, I used, during my stay at Kano, to collect plants, shrubs, insects, &c. and stuff any birds that I might happen to shoot, if I fancied there was any thing peculiar or strange in their appearance. By this means I soon acquired a great variety of beautiful insects, which, with the birds and plants, I attempted to bring to England with me; but the portmanteau in which they were placed having been frequently wetted on my return to the coast, they were all so completely spoiled, that I was obliged to throw them away.

On the 12th of November I had the happiness of receiving the following letter from my master, dated Soccasoo, Tuesday, October 26, 1826:—

"DEAR RICHARD,

"I arrived here on Thursday, after a most fatiguing and harassing journey. I find the city in much the same state as on my former visit. They say it has been burnt by the rebels of Goober, but I have observed no traces of a recent conflagration, and therefore suspect the rumour to be unfounded. Sultan Bello has been investing Coonia, the capital of Goober, with a large but irregular army. I visited him in his camp previously to my arrival here. He appeared glad to see me, and welcomed me to his country with the utmost cordiality. He is now at Magaria, anticipating an attack from the rebel chief, but is expected here shortly. The Arabs have already begun their underhand and deceitful practices, by tampering with Mohammed [an Arab servant], and insinuating the injury he would do his soul by serving an enemy to their faith. The man hardly knows how to act; on the one hand he dreads the resentment of his namesake the Prophet; and on the other, if he quits my service, he must necessarily throw himself upon the good-nature of his rascally countrymen, who indeed make golden promises, but whose filthy niggardliness is proverbial, even amongst the Falatahs. I shall certainly feel his loss severely, if Mohammed follows their advice, as I have no one in whom I can repose so much confidence as himself; but I have left it entirely to his own choice, either to go or stay. I have just had a conversation with a messenger, arrived within these few minutes from Bello and the Godado; he tells me the rebels are hourly expected near Magaria, and of his sovereign's wish for me to make all haste to him, as he is utterly unconscious how long he may be detained with his army. For the purpose of assisting me on my journey, the Sultan has sent me two camels and a horse; and most likely I shall leave this city to-morrow or next day.

"It is most violently hot here. I fancy the weather has already made some impression on my health, for I feel now and then a little feverish and unwell. I sincerely wish it may not increase upon me. Heaven knows I have had enough of sickness since I first set my foot on African soil; and it would be disheartening indeed if I should be laid up at this particular time. Let me hope your health is improved since I saw you. It would grieve me exceedingly to hear an unfavourable account of it; and I would suggest that you keep both mind and body as much employed as possible. By right you should have no idle moments. I hope you ride out every day, and amuse yourself with shooting and stuffing birds: this will tend to keep you in good health and spirits. Apply your mind strictly to the duties of religion; rely firmly on the mercy and assistance of Heaven; for in all your difficulties and distress, this alone will bear you up like a man, and render you superior to misfortune.

"I pray God to bless you; and believe me to be

"Your sincere friend and master,

"HUGH CLAPPERTON."

"*Rd. Lander, Kano.*"

Towards the latter end of November, I received a second letter from Capt. Clapperton, dated Soccasoo, November 7th, 1826. The ollowing is a copy of it:—

" DEAR RICHARD,

"I returned from Magaria yesterday: the Sultan received his present with rapture; nor did the godado appear much less pleased with his. I enjoy, thank God, tolerable health, with the exception of being afflicted at times with a sharp pain in my side, which annoys me greatly; but I hope it will soon wear off. The Sultan does not seem in the least willing for me to visit Bornou, by reason of the war; but I shall do all in my power to overturn his unjust prejudices. He fancies, no doubt, the present intended for the Sheikh consists of warlike stores; at least, I am pretty confident my kind friends the Arabs have intimated as much to him. Yet I am infinitely pleased to learn that Bello does not altogether relish their counsel, and that he judges pretty correctly of the falsehood and deceit they have so often practised to serve their own ends.

"If the road to Bornou be denied me, I really can't tell what we shall do, or how we shall get home. It is certain if we pursue a different route, my business will be incomplete, and of all things this lies nearest my heart. It is not likely, however, I shall be kept in suspense a great while longer, and I shall know with certainty perhaps in a few days. I am already heartily tired of this place; and most devoutly wish I were with you. I long to turn my face towards our dear country again; yet whenever I think calmly of it, as oftentimes I do, a cloud seems to hang over the future which saddens me, I know not why, and makes me excessively low-spirited. I would cheerfully dissipate all gloomy reflections if I could; but they come over one at times when one is least capable of resisting their influence, and an unpleasant sensation steals insensibly upon the mind, and renders one careless of oneself, and regardless of the world.

"My dear Richard, do *you* endeavour to keep up your spirits. You tell me you are ill; I imagine this proceeds more from brooding over your misfortunes than any other cause whatever: it is not well to do so; you should not suffer despondency and dejection to have the mastery over your judgment and resolution. Think of your friends in England, and fancy yourself in their little circle; never permit hope to sink so far within you, as to say to yourself, 'I shall never see my country again.' Such thoughts, I repeat, should never be indulged; for they are ever attended with mischief. Your disorder is, indeed, a peculiarly painful one; yet it is one which every European must expect to be visited with in this remote region. I have been afflicted with it myself before now, and you see I am completely recovered from its effects.

"Let me entreat you, therefore, to hope for the best: it is unmanly to repine at any trifling casualty that may befal one, which we are all so very apt to do. Above all things, place your confidence in the wisdom of the Almighty; let your whole heart and affections rest upon him, for he alone is able to support you under the trying sickness that wastes you, and conduct you in safety to dear old England. Pray to Heaven night and morning, and read the church service as often as you can, particularly on the Sabbath; for a firm reliance on the goodness and mercy of the Divine Power, will inspire you with confidence, and bear you up with cheerfulness and courage, even when all earthly enjoyments fail you. For my own part, I am inclined to believe you will soon be well, and that we shall shortly see better and happier days. Most likely I shall leave this city for Kano the latter part of the week, and surely I need not repeat how happy I shall be to see you again.

"Adieu, and believe me
    "Your sincere friend and master,
            "H. CLAPPERTON."
"*Richard Lander, Kano.*"

The above letter had been delivered to me but two days, when I received a message from the governor of Kano to pay him a visit at his house. On entering the apartment in which he was seated, he abruptly informed me that he had just received a letter from my master, which contained a wish for me to come to him immediately with all the baggage. This piece of intelligence surprised me not a little, for I had been led to believe, from the tenor of his last letter, that, instead of my proceeding to Soccasoo, Captain Clapperton must by that time have been on the road to Kano. I could not help fancying, however, that something of a melancholy nature had taken place, which, from motives of delicacy, had been prudently withheld from me, although I was at a loss to conjecture of what nature it could be; for it did not occur to me at the moment that Bello, who bore a high character for uprightness and integrity, could resort to so mean a stratagem, in order to inveigle an unprotected stranger into his power, without assigning any reason for such unwarrantable conduct.

Two days after this interview (22d November) I received another invitation from the governor, on which occasion, after briefly alluding to the former conversation, he hinted that it was necessary for me to quit the city without delay, naming the 25th as the day most proper for my departure. He said he should make my master a present of five *pack* bullocks to convey the goods to Soccasoo, and order four men to take charge of the animals on the road.

On the 24th I paid my respects to the governor, with whom I was closeted considerably more than an hour; and on rising to depart, he shook hands heartily with me, saying, with much warmth and feeling, " Good bye, 'little Christian,' God take you safe to Soccasoo." On going back to my house, I found Hat Salah rather impatiently waiting my return; he advised me to procure a strong camel by all means, affirming that the bullocks of themselves were inadequate for the purpose intended. I agreed with him in this particular, and purchased one which the Arab recommended for 62,000 cowries.

CHAPTER VIII.

The Author quits Kano to join his master—His illness on the road—Anecdotes of the natives, and his reception by them—Pasko's last robbery, and elopement—He is overtaken, and brought back—The Tuarick merchants—The Author's arrival at Soccatoo, the metropolis of the Falatah empire—Residence there—Pasko's dismissal, conduct, and marriage.

On the 25th of November I left the city of Kano, accompanied by *honest* Pasko, who had just been liberated from his confinement, Abdulfitha the Arab, and messengers from Bello and the governor of Kano. At one in the afternoon our party halted at Zungugwâ; but the camel, in endeavouring to enter by one of the narrow gates of the town, unfortunately broke two boxes, in which were contained stationery and other articles. This accident detained us outside the walls for more than an hour, when the men were obliged to take the goods on their heads, and carry them to the residence of the chief, at a distance of half a mile from the spot. I waited on him myself shortly afterwards, and gave him a pair of scissors, fifty needles, and a small paper of cloves, all which pleased him highly. The chief then led me into one of his best huts, where he told me I might remain till I felt inclined to leave the place, and shortly afterwards sent me butter, sour milk, a couple of fine fowls, with tuah and corn.

I awoke early in the morning of the 26th, and leaving the hut of the hospitable chief, after a ride of six hours, came to Markee, a large, though thinly inhabited village, the chief of which, a kind-hearted old man, upwards, I should think, of ninety years of age, and withal very feeble, was delighted to see me, and testified the pleasure he felt by repeatedly shaking hands with me for the space of half an hour; and would undoubtedly have pulled off my arm, if I had not expressed myself too greatly fatigued to stand so long a time in one place. After a short conversation, he conducted me into an inner apartment, and, bidding me to sit, took from a calabash which was suspended from the ceiling a small box made of skin, round which had been wound, with the greatest care, upwards of five hundred yards of thread, which occupied him twenty minutes in taking off. This having been done, he showed me four bits of tin lying at the bottom of the box, about the size of swan and common shot. The old chief then gave me to understand, with much seriousness, as well as earnestness of manner, that the little balls I was looking at had been given to him by an Arab fifteen years before, who had positively affirmed that they were of silver, and possessed of life. The larger pieces, the old man continued, were of the masculine, and the smaller of the feminine gender; the latter of which would produce young at the end of every twelve years, and till the expiration of that period were by no means to be looked at!

In order to impart warmth to the balls, he had enveloped them in a quantity of cotton wool, and the thread had been tied round the box, that the offspring might have no opportunity of escaping! "But," said the hoary-headed chief, with a disappointed air, "though I kept them with the utmost care, agreeably to the instructions I had received, for twelve years, to my consternation and sorrow, at the end of that period, I found that they had made no increase, and I begin to think that they never will;" in saying which, the tender-hearted man was so grievously affected that he burst into tears. It was with the greatest difficulty that I could refrain from laughing aloud in his face; but succeeded at length in subduing the strong inclination I had to be merry, and I told him, with all the solemnity the occasion required, that the Arab was a rogue and had deceived him; that the articles he had so highly valued were bits of tin, and not of silver; that they were without life, and, therefore, could not infuse the living principle into other inanimate substances. I consoled the old gentleman, however, upon the hoax that had been so successfully played off upon him, and sympathized with him in his sorrow.

His mind soon afterwards became more composed, although at times he could not help sobbing audibly; and after answering numerous questions put to me about my country, I complained of indisposition, and retired to rest.

After spending a sleepless night, I arose unrefreshed at six in the morning, and pursuing our journey, passed close to a large Falatah town, called Kiowah, in the neighbourhood of which were numerous herds of horned cattle grazing. Here, as in other parts of Houssa, the cows are mostly white, and the sheep of the same colour, spotted with red and black, which occasioned the latter animals to have a very agreeable appearance at a distance, and recalled to my memory Jacob's spotted sheep, mentioned in Scripture. In the afternoon we arrived at Guâri, a large walled town with an indifferent population. The beasts were unable to enter the gate with their loads, by reason of its narrowness, and being unwilling for the men to take them into the town on their heads, which would have occupied a considerable time—much longer, indeed, than my fatigue and illness would allow, I reposed for the night underneath the branches of a large tree. On being made acquainted with my arrival, the chief paid me a visit, and seating himself by my side, entered most familiarly into conversation with me, in the course of which he observed that tigers abounded in the neighbourhood, and unless I kept fires burning during the whole of the night, my attendants and cattle would in all probability be attacked and destroyed by those rapacious animals. He also informed me, that two years before, the Gooberites took and pillaged his town, putting to the sword nearly the whole of its inhabitants, and he himself narrowly escaped with life. This was, no doubt, the reason of the scantiness of the population, and the poverty of the chief and his remaining subjects. As soon as the chief had returned to the town, a new-married couple paid me a visit. To the bride, a very interesting girl of eighteen, I gave guinea-nuts, to the value of one hundred cowries, on accepting which she dropped on one knee, and thanked me in a modest but graceful manner; and in the evening, in return for the trifling present I had given her, she sent me some butter-milk, which was an acceptable gift at that time.

At the usual hour, on the morning of the 28th, we again set out, and halted at a small wretched looking village, called Kookay, at twelve at noon. The inhabitants, who were as squalid in appearance as their village was contemptible, were miserably attired, and complained sadly, amongst other grievances, of the mischief done to their crops by repeated visits of wild pigs, which had completely destroyed the principal part of them.

At noon of the next day we stopped at Duncammee, a moderately sized walled town, with an overflowing population. I was both surprised and pleased to observe the neatness of this town, and the tidiness of its inhabitants. Every inch of spare ground was planted with tobacco, and tastefully fenced round with the dried stalks of that plant. The inhabitants at the northern quarter of the town manufacture large quantities of cotton cloths, which are neat and durable. The wall, by which the town is surrounded, was in a decayed state, but the houses were in excellent condition. The chief welcomed me to his dwelling, and offered me the best apartment in it; and to remunerate his generosity I gave him a clasp knife and a hundred needles.

On the morning of the 30th we were again in motion, and halted at Gaza at noon. The chief, like his neighbours, was happy to see me, lodged me in his own house, and paid every attention to my wants.

Next day we continued our journey at the usual hour, and halted at Royoó at one o'clock at noon. In that town I became suddenly worse, lost my sight in an extraordinary manner, and could not rise in bed from excessive weakness and pain. Fancying I should be able to proceed no further, and that my existence was drawing rapidly to a close, I called Pasko to my bedside, and implored him, after he had buried me, to take particular care of the property he would be left in charge of, and travel with the utmost expedition to Soccasoo, where he would be rewarded, according to his deserts, by Captain Clapperton; for thief and villain as he had proved himself to be, he had some good points, and I thought that the oath he had taken before the Governor of Kano would have bound him to honesty.

On the 1st of December I remained dreadfully ill, expecting every moment to draw my last breath; but at two o'clock on the afternoon of the next day I rallied a little, and although unable to sit up, determined to see my dear master, if possible, before I died. With this object in view, I ordered my people to prepare a couch for me on the back of the camel, after which they lifted me gently into it, and I almost immediately desired them to proceed.

The Chief of Royoó, who was one of Bello's principal fighting men, behaved particularly kindly to me, and I really believe sincerely sympathized in my distress. He expressed his regret and sorrow at parting with me in so languid a state, and intimated, that it would be dangerous to go on, although he did not oppose my resolution, when he saw it would be useless to do so. The path, the greater part of the way, being very narrow, and thickly lined on each side with a species of prickly thorn, I was annoyed greatly, in consequence of their sharp points frequently tearing the covering from my bed, and exposing my body to the intense heat of a burning sun. The Kano messenger, however, ascertaining the cause of my uneasiness, and compassionating my misery, rode before the camel, and with the greatest dexterity lopped off the overhanging branches that were likely to impede the animal's progress, which rendered the remaining part of the journey infinitely more tolerable. The violent shaking of the camel caused a faintness to come over me several times on the road, on which occasions my party uniformly halted until I revived; and in this manner we travelled till seven in the evening, when we entered the walled town of Koólefée.

The chief, a remarkably fine old man, never having seen a white man, was in transports the moment he learnt I was in the town; and running to the camel, he took me from off its back, and carried me into an apartment which had been hastily prepared for my reception. Placing me on a mat, he took a goora nut from his pocket, and holding it betwixt his finger and thumb, intreated me to chew one end of it, in order that he might have the honor of eating with a white man, and a Christian; this I succeeded in doing after some difficulty, when he immediately ate the remainder with much apparent satisfaction. His great men, who surrounded me, reproved the chief sharply for doing this; but quickly answering them in a pleasant and firm tone, he said that he believed the "Little Christian" was as good a man as himself, or any of them; which effectually silenced their remarks. The chief shortly afterwards went out, and returning in a few minutes with a bowl containing six quarts of new milk, sweetened with honey, told me that he was determined to see me swallow the whole of it before he left the apartment. Contrary to his wishes, however, I partook sparingly of the contents of the bowl at first, but during the night took large and repeated draughts, which refreshed and invigorated me.

On arising the following morning, I found myself so much better, that I travelled on horseback, although not without much difficulty, to Zunko, a miserable village in which we slept.

At sunrise on the 4th, we resumed our journey, and after a fatiguing ride of seven hours, arrived at Roma, a town insignificant as to size, but which being built on an eminence, commands a delightful prospect of the country for miles round. As soon as I entered the house of the chief, in which I slept, he made me the accustomed presents of provisions, &c. for which he accepted in return a pair of scissars, a hundred needles, and a paper of cloves. Several Falatah girls of a bright copper colour; came to me in the evening, who were exceedingly beautiful, having delicate and graceful forms; and, with a curiosity so natural to their sex, were all eager to catch a glimpse of the " Little Christian," they having before seen the " *Great* Christian," as my master was called. In the course of the afternoon some of these damsels brought me milk and butter, for which I requited them with a few glass beads. In the night, I was rejoiced to find that my disorder, from the effects of which I had suffered so greatly, left me entirely: and from that hour my health rapidly and wonderfully improved.

We bade adieu to the chief of Roma early in the morning of the fifth, and arrived at a contemptible village, called Bogell, in the course of the afternoon. Having slept there, we pursued our journey on the following day, and on entering Zulamee, the chief capered for joy on welcoming me to his town, and ordered four men to guard the beasts and property. A band of robbers having infested the neigbourhood for some time, had committed serious depredations on the inhabitants; and the chief, fancying that if the goods were left unprotected, they would be stolen, desired me to discharge a gun morning and evening, that the brigands might not think I was unprepared to receive them. They did not, however, think proper to molest me; but the King of Kashna was not quite so fortunate, for on the preceding day a fine horse was stolen from him, which he never afterwards recovered. I remained at Zulamee two days, in order to recruit the spirits of the party, and refresh the animals under their charge.

We quitted the town on the morning of the

ninth, and sleeping at Gundumowah, a small but neat Falatah village, arrived at Sansanee on the following day. The country traversed was thickly wooded, and the path lay for three hours through a large bush, which having recently been visited by a horde of elephants, the impressions of whose feet were very perceptible, travelling was rendered extremely unpleasant, and even dangerous. On our arrival the chief of the town ordered an open shed, occupied by a number of calves, to be cleaned out for our reception. In the evening, placing the baggage in the centre, I desired the men to lie around it, whilst I reposed near the most valuable articles. Not deeming the property sufficiently secure in so exposed a place, my sleep was rather disturbed; and arising about ten or eleven o'clock in the night, I found that my camel had strayed from outside the shed. Being unwilling to arouse my drowsy companions, I went myself in quest of him; and on returning a short time afterwards, discovered, to my infinite surprise and alarm, that Pasko had decamped with a valuable gun, two pistols, a cutlass, six sovereigns, nineteen dollars, twenty large and small knives, and various other articles, which he had contrived to extract from the boxes in which they had been secured. To deceive me, the artful old scoundrel had put a pillow into a sack, over which he threw an old tobe, and laid it along his own mat. On the discovery I instantly made an alarm, and sent to the chief for a dozen armed horsemen to go in pursuit of the robber.

As I was standing in the shed in the afternoon of the next day, I perceived a party of horsemen coming towards me at full gallop. On approaching within a few yards they suddenly checked their steeds, and brandishing their spears over their heads, exclaimed in a loud voice, " Nasarah, Nasarah, acqui de moogoo!" (Christian, Christian, we have the rogue!) The men informed me that a little before daybreak in the morning, hearing the report of a gun, they rode towards the spot whence the sound seemed to proceed, and saw Pasko perched on the top of a high tree, the stolen articles lying at the root of it. On their threatening to shoot him with poisoned arrows unless he immediately came down, the old fellow hastily obeyed the summons, and delivered himself into their hands without uttering a syllable. One of the horsemen took the trembling scoundrel behind him, and the whole party instantly clapped spurs to their horses, and rode swiftly towards the village. I asked Pasko what had possessed him to abscond in so disgraceful a manner after all the protestations he had made to serve me with fidelity. He replied, that as his countrymen, the Gooberites, were at war with the Falatahs, he was afraid the latter would cut off his head the moment he was recognized in Soccasoo, and therefore he had adopted the wiser plan of securing his person from danger by running away. Whilst he was speaking the chief of the village, running up to us, cried out, " A blessing, a blessing! you have caught the thief, let me take off his head!" Not wishing to gratify the *good-natured* Falatah in this his merciful request, I took the punishment of Pasko into my own hands; and it being his third or fourth offence, I ordered him to be heavily ironed, and pinioned in the town dungeon. This sentence was rigidly enforced, and on the following day, the criminal having expressed a wish to speak to me, I sent for him. He came into my hut, and holding up his naked arms, which were swollen to thrice their natural size, begged so piteously to be liberated from his confinement, or at least to have his punishment mitigated in some degree, that I desired he might not be pinioned again, as that operation seemed to have given him most pain; but his irons were not taken off till our departure from the place.

On the 13th, five hundred camels, laden with salt, obtained from the borders of the Desert, entered Sansanee, preceded by their owners, a party of twenty Tuarick merchants, whose appearance was singularly novel and imposing. The men were all attired in the same fashion, and mounted on handsome pied camels, which trotted into the town with uncommon speed. Their dress consisted of black cotton tobes, and full trousers of the same colour;

white caps encircled with black turbans, which concealed every part of the face but the nose and eyes; and red morocco boots. In the right hand they held a long and highly-polished spear, whilst the left was occupied in grasping their shields (the only defensive armour with which the Tuaricks are acquainted), and retaining the reins of the camels. The shields were covered with white leather, and ornamented with a small plate of silver in the centre. As they passed me they shook their lances, which glittered in the sun-beams, and their appearance was certainly warlike and formidable in the extreme. Stopping suddenly in front of the chief's house, they all exclaimed, as if with one voice, " Tchow!" at the sound whereof the camels fell simultaneously on their knees, and the riders dismounted to pay their respects. They came in a body to see me shortly afterwards, and notwithstanding their apparent respectability, evinced not the slightest unwillingness to beg money of me, which they did in a most importunate manner. One of the merchants, yet more incessant in his solicitations than his companions, amongst other shining qualities he affirmed he was in possession of, stated with the utmost seriousness, that he was " God's own slave," and on that account he was not to be overlooked. I said that the Almighty loved his servants, and made them prosperous and happy, and therefore he stood in no need of my assistance. The fellow, however, would not be repulsed, but continued hanging on me, and in fact almost tore the clothes from my back, till out of all patience, I took the importunate slave by the shoulders, and thrust him out of the shed into the street. As he went off, no doubt greatly humiliated in his own estimation, he muttered some reproaches which I could not comprehend, and said that I was the first person he had ever applied to in vain for money. Like thousands of others, these merchants were very inquisitive, and amongst other questions, wished to know whether many of my countrymen had not tails like monkeys! I assured them that no human being had that elegant appendage; but instead of believing my assertion, they shook their heads, looked wise, and said,

"You do not speak the truth, white man, we know better than you;" on saying which, they surveyed me with more attention than before, and one amongst them walked round me several times, cautiously raising the end of my tobe, to ascertain with certainty whether I had any thing in the shape of a tail! On observing the man's motions, I took off my tobe, which convinced his countrymen that *I* at least was without a tail, when they appeared better satisfied; and left my shed in the course of an hour to look after their wives and children, who were with the camels on the road, and had not then arrived.

Provisions being rather scarce, I went a-shooting on the 14th, to procure a few pigeons for dinner. The Tuarick men, women, and children, on hearing the report of my gun, surrounded me in great numbers, and were infinitely amazed to see the birds falling dead at my feet from the tops of the tall trees. After examining them with the greatest attention, they declared that I was a beautiful man, too good a one for a Kaffir, and that I ought to be a worshipper of the true faith.

In the afternoon of the 16th, fifty armed horsemen, sent by Bello, arrived at Sansanee, to accompany me to Soccasoo, his capital, in which he was waiting my arrival with impatience, and urged me to prepare to accompany them. The soldiers had brought my master's two camels to assist in conveying the goods, which animals, as I subsequently learnt, the Godado had borrowed under false pretences. A messenger belonging to the Governor of Kano, who had accompanied the escort so far on his way to that city, came to me in the evening, unobserved by the Falatahs, and gave me a letter from Captain Clapperton, of which the following is a transcript:

"*Soccasoo, Wednesday, Dec.* 13, 1826.

" Dear Richard,

" I hope you do well; I am still here, contrary to my expectations, and Heaven knows when I shall be permitted to leave. This cursed Bornou war has overturned all my plans and intentions, and set the minds of the people generally against me, as it is pretty well understood by both rich and poor, that I have presents for their enemy the Sheikh. I wish, with all my heart, it was ended; no matter whether the Falatahs or Bornouese be victorious, so I could conveniently pursue my journey. The Sultan has told me that I may return by way of Bornou, if I insist upon it, but raises so many obstacles, that it amounts to a prohibition. He is evidently unwilling for me to have any dealings with his adversaries. I do not know how this matter will end; I must acknowledge I do not like the appearance of things just now; God grant my fears may be groundless. Since my last I have been seriously ill with an enlargement of the spleen,* but am now much relieved from the pain attendant upon this complaint; and the swelling is also greatly reduced. I amuse myself as often as opportunities occur, which are seldom enough, and frequently take a ramble through the town, or a ride into the country. I generally feel stronger after the exercise, and would recommend you to adopt a

* In some counties in England called " ague-cake," and supposed to arise from the effects of intermittent fevers.

similar practice, for, believe me, you would soon experience the benefit of it. Three or four fires have happened here lately, which have done much mischief; but nothing of mine, I am happy to say, has been injured by them, although a house almost adjoining ours has been burnt to the ground. People say the rebels of Goober are the authors of them, but I put no confidence in these rumours, as they are without the slightest proof. I believe I have nothing more, in the shape of news, to acquaint you with, and my only reason for writing you at all is, to let you know how I get on, that you may not be uneasy on my account. Adieu, Richard, and rest assured I have your interest and welfare at heart.

" Your sincere friend and master,
" Hugh Clapperton."
" *Richard Lander, Kano.*"

I was astonished, on perusing this letter, to find that my master knew nothing of the circumstance of my having left Kano, still less of my being so near him; and it struck me forcibly at the time that Bello wished to get me into his power, only to become the sole possessor of the presents intended for the Sheikh of Bornou, by laying violent hands both on Captain Clapperton and myself. With this belief I arose next morning, and asked the Godado's brother, who commanded the escort, if it was not the Sultan's intention to take away our lives on my entering Soccasoo, as my master knew nothing of what had transpired; but the Falatah answered,— " Fear nothing, our King will not injure either of you; his sole reason for sending for you is, that as he has seen but one Christian, he feels the greatest desire to become acquainted with a second." " Remember the men of Boussa!" I simply retorted, when he left me in extreme haste and great uneasiness.

The Godado's brother was as importunate as the Tuarick merchants in begging money of me to purchase goora nuts, for the two first days after the arrival of the escort, and became so troublesome that I at length told him I had no property of my own, but that all he saw belonged to my master, without whose consent I was determined not to spare a single cowry. The Falatah was not at all pleased at the answer; but on telling him that on my arrival in Soccasoo he should be handsomely rewarded, he ceased to plague me.

Every thing being in readiness, on the 19th, I liberated old Pasko, who seemed dispirited, and truly sorry for the offence he had been guilty of, and at two in the afternoon I quitted the town with the escort, but was obliged to leave a bullock behind, the animal being lamed, and unable to walk a hundred steps without stumbling. Having travelled at a rapid rate through the dreaded " Goober Bush," we arrived, much fatigued, at Magaria, about eleven o'clock the next night. The poor horses and camels having suffered dreadfully during the journey from thirst and over-exertion, we were obliged to remain in the town two days, in order that they might enjoy a little rest. During our stay I resided in a house belonging to the Godado, whose brother supplied me with abundance of excellent provisions. I was requested by some of the principal inhabitants to kill a few birds with my gun, that several strangers then in the town might have an opportunity of seeing in what manner they were procured in my country. I soon gratified their curiosity, by shooting a small bird at the distance of fifty yards; on which they betrayed the utmost surprise, nor would they believe for a long time that it was really dead, but kept turning it round, and feeling whether it had actually received a wound.

On the 23rd we quitted the town of Magaria, and, to my great joy, entered Soccasoo about two o'clock in the afternoon of the same day, after a disagreeable and wearisome journey (from Kano) of nearly a month. Not having seen my master for the period of a quarter of a year, I made the greatest haste to his house; but not finding him at home, I was conducted to the Godado's, with whose owner I found him in earnest conversation. Although certainly surprised, he was glad to see me, and we walked home together.

The day after my arrival (24th December), Sultan Bello sent a messenger to request my master and myself to repair without delay to his residence. As soon as we were admitted into his presence, he abruptly began the conversation by inquiring the nature of the presents I had with me, and was extremely solicitous to know if I had left any of them behind in Kano, for the Sheikh of Bornou. I replied that I had not. "Are you sure of that?" rejoined the Sultan. I answered with firmness a second time in the negative. Bello then demanded the King of England's letters to the Sheikh, which my master, after a short pause, reluctantly produced; but vehemently opposed the Sultan's wishes for him to open and read them, observing, that as soon as his sovereign should discover, on his return to England, that he had so unfaithfully broken his trust, he would instantly be beheaded. The Falatah prince then took the letters into his own hands, and on his graciously waving his hand in token that he wished to have nothing more to say, we bowed, and left the apartment.

We had not returned to our hut a great while, when the Godado, his brother, Hat Sallah, (who had received secret instructions to overtake me on the road,) with several of the principal inhabitants of Soccasoo, entered, and demanded, in the name of the Sultan, the presents intended for the Sheikh of Bornou, together with all the arms and ammunition which we should not want ourselves. My master became violently agitated when their errand was communicated, and rising from the mat on which he had been reposing, exclaimed with energy and bitterness :—

"There is no faith in any of you; you are an unjust people; you are worse than highway robbers!"

The Falatahs cautioned him to be more moderate in his expressions, or it might cost him his head.

"If I lose my head," retorted the Captain, in the same determined tone and manner, "it will be for no other crime than that of speaking for the just rights of my king and country; I repeat, you are a nation of scoundrels and robbers."

Hat Sallah entreated him (in Arabic) to express himself with less emphasis, and in milder language before the people, who would carry every word he had uttered to their sovereign.

I also joined in the same request, and begged him, as the attempt at resistance, for people so circumstanced as we were, would be the height of imprudence, to accede to the commands of the sultan, how tyrannical soever they might be. At length, after much persuasion, Capt. Clapperton consented that the presents in question should be produced; but desired the godado, on his leaving the apartment, to inform his king that he never wished to see him again; and that his business with him, after such perfidious conduct, was at an end.

A short time after they had quitted our house, Mallam Mudey returned with a message from Bello, stating it to be the intention of that monarch to write to his *friend* the King of England, in explanation of his behaviour; but my master assured the holy man that *his* sovereign would not even look at the superscription of a letter from Bello, after being made acquainted with the dastardly action by which he had so disgraced himself.

Soccasoo has been considerably enlarged by the present sultan, and is indisputably the most important city in the interior of Africa. The wall that surrounds the capital of the Falatah empire, does not indeed encompass so large a portion of ground as that of Kano, but its population is treble the amount; and allowing the latter city to contain forty thousand souls, the aggregate number of inhabitants in Soccasoo will be one hundred and twenty thousand; which computation I do not conceive to be over-rated.

Kano is distant from Soccasoo twenty regular days journey, or about two hundred and fifty English miles. The metropolis is built in a pleasant situation, on the summit of a gently elevated spot of land, and has a river flowing near the northern end, which enters the Quorra four days journey from Cubbé. The wall is high, and provided with eleven gates; but has an extremely heavy appearance. Architecture, as a science, is not cultivated in the interior; and the termites can rear as elegant a mansion as the natives, and in a far more ingenious manner. The habitations in Soccasoo are constructed like those of Kano, with clay, and have a dull, gloomy appearance.

An old Haussan with two asses arrived in the city one day from Egypt. Having stopped in the different towns through which he had to pass, for the purpose of trafficking with their inhabitants, he had accomplished the long and dangerous journey in little more than a twelvemonth. He informed me that he had undergone great privations on the road, and had well nigh perished of thirst on more than one occasion. He had had no human companion to cheer him; and his affection for the brute associates of his lonely pilgrimage was singularly great. They had fared in common with himself; they had eaten and slept together; and, said the old man, as he drove away the patient-looking animals, "I would as soon lose my life as be deprived of them." The Haussan observed that it was his intention to proceed to Tombuctoo the following week, and that on his return he should pay me a visit, but I never saw or heard any thing of him afterwards.

The people of Soccasoo cry their provisions round the city; and milk, fish, &c. are daily hawked through the streets by the lower orders, whose voices are as loud and shrill as those heard in London. The cry of "*Nono de mi!*" (milk and butter) always put me in mind of bells belonging to village churches; there was something peculiarly plaintive in the rising and falling of the voice of the young female who used to vend those articles morning and evening in the immediate neighbourhood of our dwelling; and, in my opinion, it strikingly resembled them in sound. "Namah du tonkah," mutton (literally "flesh of the sheep"); "Namah de la comma" (camel's meat); "Namah du acquia" (beef); "Gorassa" (little cakes made of pounded wheat); are also cried every morning; as is likewise "dowah," and every other variety of grain produced in Haussa.

Wheat was first imported into Haussa by the Arabs about a century ago; and even now they have the exclusive cultivation of it. Bread is only to be met with in two cities, Soccasoo and Zaria, and is manufactured by the female slaves of the Arabs, who sell it publicly by retail for their masters. For a very good reason I never tasted any of it whilst in Africa, and therefore can say nothing as to its good or bad quality.

Pasko, whom my master had dismissed his service the moment he was made acquainted with his two-fold villainy, without paying the wages that were due to him, applied to a native lawyer in Soccasoo for advice; but the learned Falatah having patiently listened to the details of his case, discarded him, with the assurance, that if he had been Abdullah (Captain Clapperton's travelling name), instead of rewarding him, he would have cut off his head!

Under this consolation the old man, having a small sum of money in his possession, turned snuff-merchant, but being cheated by every body, became insolvent in the course of a very short time, and, in order to procure a slender maintenance, was ultimately obliged to cut wood from a neighbouring forest. In the height of his prosperity as a tradesman, Pasko, forgetting all his former vows and misfortunes, and contrary to his usual custom, formally paid his addresses to a black slave, named Mattah Gewow (literally Miss, or woman-elephant), in the household of Ben Gumso, an Arab. This woman, a native of Yariba, which country is notorious for ugly females, had a countenance inexpressibly hideous, but was well known by all ranks in Soccasoo, as the most experienced maker of *tuah** which that or any other city could produce. In addition to the other attractions of this lady, a huge white tooth hung from her upper jaw, affectionately embracing the nether lip; and her chin was bristled most divinely with a slender but conspicuous and stubborn beard,—she being the only individual of her sex I had seen in the country possessing so masculine an ornament. Mattah Gewow was in the decline of life, having seen between fifty and sixty dry seasons pass over her head, and had, in her earlier years, been allured from the paths of innocence and virtue by a blind fiddler in the pay of the late and present sultan, who had refused to make her reparation by marriage. From that period to the time of our visiting Soccasoo, no sable swain had been emboldened

* A kind of pudding made of flour, butter, and eggs.

to pay her any marked attentions; and the injured woman was inconsolable under the thoughts of living for ever in " single blessedness," when the affectionate Pasko, having casually partaken of her far-famed tuah, pronounced it to be the best he had ever tasted, and immediately offered his heart and person, which, after a few *invisible* blushes on the lady's part, were modestly accepted. The betrothed, as soon as they perfectly understood each other, spent all their leisure moments in their own delightful society, Pasko extolling the charms of the peerless Miss Elephant to the skies, and Miss Elephant returning the compliment by perpetually discovering fresh subjects for admiration and love in the person and physiognomy of the incomparable snuff-merchant. Thus the first few evenings of their courtship were passed, at which time I was a constant visiter at Ben Gumso's, and often overheard their tender discourse. I broke in upon the lovers one day rather unexpectedly, in the midst of their dalliance, when Pasko was pouring out an eloquent and passionate eulogium on the graces of his Mattah, who, on observing me,

"*Blush'd* at the praise of her own loveliness!"

and, with her adorer, looked exceedingly foolish. Being unwilling to disturb the harmony that had prevailed before my intrusion, I left the happy couple to enjoy themselves as they thought proper, and quitted the house.

A day having been fixed upon for the marriage ceremony, the suitor determined to spend it jovially; and his own finances being at a very low ebb, he borrowed four thousand cowries of Ben Gumso, in order that nothing might be wanting to stamp dignity and consequence on the celebration of the festival. Pasko had just before embraced Islamism, and rigidly observed the outward rules of that belief; besides which he was well skilled in all the learning and knowledge of the Falatahs; so that the Arab did not hesitate to advance him the money he sought, on the faith of his bare promise of re-payment. The evening preceding the ceremony, Pasko sent a present of snuff, an old shirt, &c. to Mattah, which was acknowleged by a bowl of rich tuah; and the compact was thus formally ratified. On the following morning the " fatha" was read, and Pasko and the *lovely* Mattah became man and wife. Agreeably to promise, the **happy** bridegroom spent the day merrily with a friend or two he had invited; but so far forgot himself, his newly-adopted religion, and the respect he owed his bride, that towards evening he became intoxicated; indeed so much so that he was bereaved of his reason; and Mattah, who was only *tipsy*, perceiving her husband in this pickle, was very wrath, and pouring a whole bowl of hot half-boiled tuah over his head, face, and breast, gave him a sound drubbing with an empty calabash, and turned the unfortunate snuff-merchant out into the street half dead, where he remained in a state of insensibility till the next morning. On awaking, and finding himself bespattered from head to foot with tuah, Pasko had a confused recollection of the preceding evening's debauch, and its disastrous consequences; but instead of disturbing the slumbers of his amiable wife, he strolled listlessly towards our hut, sorely distressed in mind and body, where I met him an hour or so afterwards, the end of his tobe being completely saturated with his tears, which were yet flowing, and his whole appearance looking uncommonly grotesque. After making me acquainted with the melancholy tale of his mishap, he begged me to use my influence in order to compromise matters betwixt his gentle consort and himself, and assured me that if I succeeded, when occasion needed, he would cheerfully lay down his life for me.

Wishing to be better acquainted with a woman, whose excessive ugliness and skilful tuah-making were the table talk of the whole kingdom of Houssa, I willingly embraced the proposition, and making a visit to Ben Gumso's, had the good fortune to reconcile the angry lady to her sorrowing lord, after which they lived very happily together, till Pasko's bankruptcy broke in upon their domestic felicity, and drove the ill-fated man into the woods. To the credit of

Mattah, however, be it spoken, she did not abandon her husband in his mournful reverse of fortune; but, with an attachmeut worthy of her sex, supplied him, as far as she was able, with food and raiment; and their parting interview, on Pasko's leaving Soccatoo with me, was beyond description natural, tender, and pathetic.

CHAPTER IX.

Religion—Laws—Government—Amusements, &c. of the Natives from Badagry to Soccatoo—Slavery in the interior countries—Timidity of the people—State of the arts amongst them—Dry and wet seasons.

THE religion of the natives from Badagry to Soccatoo is either Mohammedism or Paganism; or, as it frequently appeared to us, a mixture of both, so nicely blended, as to make it impossible to ascertain with accuracy which belief had the ascendancy. Idols, or figures of birds, beasts, and reptiles, are worshipped in Badagry, Jannah, and Yaribas exclusively, while in the kingdoms of Borghoo, Nyffé, and Houssa, Islamism prevails in a greater or less degree.

The professors of the former faith have a vague and indistinct notion of one great Being reigning above the skies, who is infinitely superior to every other in the nature of his attributes, and the extent of his power and influence. To this unknown God they pay divine adoration, through the medium of insignificant and inanimate objects, by the offering up of sacrifices to the latter, under the belief that the Great Spirit exists at so immeasurable a distance from them, and his time is so much employed in other and more important matters, that he cannot listen to the prayers of every individual. In consequence of this he appoints innumerable subordinate agents and machines, who aid and assist him, and minister to the affairs of mankind. They believe also in the existence of a powerful malevolent Spirit, who endeavours to counteract the good deeds of the Most High by every means, and is the author of all the mischief that annoys them. The people stand in the greatest dread of the power and machinations of this terrible demon, and strive to avert his wrath, and conciliate his favour, by oblations of dogs, sheep, and, in many cases, of human beings. Fetish-huts are the temples of their worship, which are regarded with superstitious awe by rich and poor; and are each furnished with one or more priests, who alone are acquainted with the mysteries of their religion. Some of the people are very sincere in their devotional exercises, which are energetic and simple; whilst many pay little respect to the exterior forms of worship, openly ridiculing those who profess a greater share of sanctity than themselves; and, whenever they are unsuccessful in their pursuits and enterprizes, even belabour their household gods without mercy. They entertain also an idea that the soul hovers round the scenes it had known in the body, for an indefinite length of time; but that it is ultimately conducted to a place of happiness or misery; a kind of heaven for the peaceable, and hell for the turbulent, according to the deeds it has suggested in this life, and there to remain everlastingly. Both Mohammedan and Pagan attach miraculous qualities to fetishes or charms, which to them are an effectual panoply against every danger; sometimes a chief or great man is actually covered with them from head to foot, and in this state considers himself as secure as Achilles in his armour. I have often been urged to discharge a pistol, loaded with ball, at the breast of an individual thus supernaturally defended, but it is unnecessary to say that I never risked the men's lives at the expence of their ignorance and credulity, having endeavoured in every instance, although unsuccessfully, to persuade them out of their superstitious prejudices by less dangerous experiments. The natives appear to have no gloomy foreboding as the hour of death approaches; nor do they, as I had often been given to understand, anticipate dissolution with any symptoms of fear or alarm.

Those who profess the Mohammedan religion amongst the negroes are as ignorant and superstitious as their idolatrous brethren; nor does it appear that their having adopted a new creed has either improved their manners, or bettered their state and condition in life. On the contrary, I have generally found the followers of the Prophet to be less hospitable to strangers, less kind to each other, and infinitely more mischievous and wicked than the heathen portions of the community, whom they, whimsically enough, affect to despise as rude barbarians, although *their* claims to superior intelligence are grounded simply on the oral communications of the principles of the Koran, received from time to time from the wandering Moors and Arabs; or from traditionary legends of their country. The artful Arabian, however, withholds from them a full half of the little he himself may be acquainted with, taking care to teach them no more than is absolutely necessary to promote his own views, and enlarge his own interests. The Mohammedan negroes go through their ablutions regularly, and when water is not to be obtained, make use of sand, as the Koran enjoins. The Tuaricks, or "Bereberes," (Children of the Desert,) adopt the latter method on all occasions, the trouble of applying water, even when they have abundance within their reach, being too irksome and unpleasant for them.

The Falatahs, who profess Islamism, understand and make use of a few Arabic prayers, but the negro that can utter so long a sentence as : "*La illah el Allah rasoul allahi!*" (There is but one God, and Mohammed is his prophet,) is styled *mallam*, or learned, and is regarded with looks of respect and reverence by his less intelligent countrymen. These mallams are scattered in great numbers over the country, and procure an easy and respectable subsistence by making fetishes, or writing charms on bits of wood, which are washed off carefully into a bason, and drunk with avidity by the credulous multitude, who consider the dirty water used in the operation as a panacea for every disease and affliction. As the office of mallam, which answers to that of priest in Catholic countries, is one of great sanctity as well as considerable emolument, every one burns with impatience to get initiated into its sacred mysteries, and enjoy a like comfortable and indolent life as the mallams themselves; for a learned man never toils or spins, but is bountifully fed, and pampered in luxury by his lay countrymen. Every caravan is furnished with one or more of these corpulent drones, who loll at their ease, while their employers are at the same time, perhaps, actually killing themselves with over-exertion.

Few of the negroes can articulate in Arabic

more than the word " Allah," or " Bismillah," believing that the frequent repetition of the former of these expressions can absolve them from all sin, without any further demonstration of their zeal and sincerity. Even after the committal of a capital offence, should the criminal be almost immediately executed, and " Allah!" is heard to tremble on his closing lips, the multitude firmly believe that his soul will inevitably be conveyed to the third Heaven, and be happy for evermore.

Swarms of sheriffs, or emirs, the real or fictitious descendants of Mohammed and Ali, have crossed the desert, and practice their disgraceful impositions to so great an extent, that the eyes of the natives are partially opened to their chicanery, and they are often regarded as characters with whom it would be dangerous to meddle.

The belief in the " Evil Eye," is equally common with Mohammedan as Pagan, and this superstition, borrowed from the Moors, has lost none of its fearful interest by being transplanted to a foreign soil. If sickness of any kind visits a child before it has attained the age of three or four years, then say the people the "Evil Eye, is fixed upon it," and the relatives of the afflicted infant endeavour to avert the wasting glance of the malevolent and unseen spirit by sacrifices of birds, and various other means.

Mallams from Houssa reside in almost every town of consequence through which we passed on our journey into the interior,—propagating their religion, and teaching the inhabitants to read and write as much as they themselves know. The Mohammedan faith is spreading daily and rapidly by this means, particularly in Nyffé, hundreds of the natives of that kingdom having lost sight of their ancient prejudices, and the religion of their forefathers, and embraced the more congenial tenets of Islamism. In some cities or towns, however, these mallams have been very roughly handled by the people, and many of them have lost their lives in disseminating, with too great eagerness, their opinions amongst the worshippers of idols. As an instance of this, five holy men, two or three of whom were Arab emirs, visited Katunga, the capital of Yariba, a few years since, and immediately began to spread the dogmas of their faith amongst the inhabitants, publicly teaching their children to read the Koran, &c. The priests of the fetish, who, in regard to their religious observances, surprizingly resemble the Druids of England before the Conquest, became sensibly alarmed at the rapid progress of another and strange belief, so inimical to their best interests, and tending to the injury, if not the complete overthrow, of the power and influence which they themselves and their ancestors had exercised for a series of ages over the minds and actions of the votaries of Paganism. They went in a body to their monarch, the present king, threatening him with the loss of his empire, if he persisted in tolerating the religious principles broached by the mallams. This denunciation so intimidated the superstitious prince, that he was frightened into a compliance with their wishes of appointing a day, or rather night, for the assassination of the unsuspecting Mussulmans, which was accordingly carried into execution, and Ben Gumso, my old friend in Soccatoo, was the only one amongst the number who escaped with life. This learned Arab was indebted to one of the wives of his Yaribean majesty, for his flight and preservation. Having overheard part of the conversation between her royal consort and the fetish-priests, and entertaining some share of veneration for the expounders of a doctrine she secretly approved of, as well as feeling compassion for them, in consequence of their premeditated massacre, the queen embraced the earliest opportunity of apprizing Ben Gumso of the danger that threatened his companions and himself; but this being done only a few seconds before the execution of the sentence, the Arab was obliged to elope in a state of nudity from his house, without having leisure to bestow a single thought on his ill-fated associates.

From that period a mallam has never ventured to enter the gates of Katunga, and the Mohammedan religion was soon forgotten by the people. They have, however, penetrated beyond the empire of Yariba, two Houssa holy men, having found their way to Jannah, the town in which Dr. Morrison, it is said, died and was buried, and three others to Badagry; but more of these individuals are allowed openly to profess their religion, or teach the children of the inhabitants to read, on pain of death; and, they are, moreover, looked upon with the greatest suspicion. The mallams, in the latter city, were not permitted to make themselves known to us on our journey into the interior, nor to me on my return, till after I had swallowed the fetish-water, when they visited me with presents of fowls, ducks, and rice, and testified the sincerest pleasure on my answering their earnest interrogations respecting their native country.

Nevertheless, in the course of a generation or two, I have no doubt, in spite of every obstacle, that the religion of Mohammed, in its exterior forms and ceremonies at least, will be universally adopted in Western and Central Africa, to the complete discomforture of the fetish-priests and their proselytes; and unless some unforseen convulsion arrest the hasty and gigantic strides Islamism is making towards that consummation, and divert the minds of the people to other objects, the period does not seem to be very remote when Paganism will be unknown in the land.

LAWS.

In a rude state of society nothing can be more simple than the laws and punishments of the people. In several of the Pagan countries of the interior of Africa, having no written code, the natives appoint elders to administer justice, at the head of whom the King, or chief, generally presides. In petty cases, such as trifling assaults and other misdemeanors, the parties concerned compromise the matter without referring it to the general assembly. In Badagry the fetish-priests are the sole judges of the people, and the statutes of their country, like those of the Druids, are recorded in their own breasts only, consequently they are mostly swayed in their decisions by interest, or influenced by prejudice and passion; but in no instance are they murmured against by either plaintiff or defendant.

Murder, adultery, and theft, are the most general crimes, and in many African countries are punishable with death, banishment, or perpetual imprisonment. In Yariba and Nyffé, the relatives of a murdered man may, and often do, accept of a sum of money, named by them, from the criminal, which is considered equivalent to corporal punishment. In Badagry, Borghoo, and Houssa, however, an individual guilty of slaying a free man, if apprehended, instantly loses his life, and his body is left to be devoured by vultures.

In cases of adultery, the injured husband is at liberty to do what he pleases with his unfaithful partner, even to the taking away her life; and if her seducer has not money enough at his disposal to satisfy the former for the loss of his honor, the same punishment may be inflicted upon him also. The extreme rigor of the laws on this head occasions instances of adultery to be exceedingly rare in every other country but Borghoo, where the punishment attending it being infinitely less rigidly exacted, the offence is more generally prevalent.

Theft, in Nyffé, is punished by imprisonment of the party or parties; and in all aggravated cases the criminal is confined in irons, in a large gloomy dungeon, for a given number of years, where he is compelled to labour in various avocations till the expiration of the term expressed in his sentence. In Yariba the crime of stealing, owing to the dreadful severity of punishment that awaits delinquents, is by no means common among the people. Free men, found guilty of larceny, are operated upon, and retained by the king or his chiefs as guardians for their numerous wives. In this state they are equal in value to five prime slaves; and it makes no difference if the thief be the father of a large family, or the husband of many females, and respectable as to wealth and connections,—the sentence is on all occasions rigorously enforced. Those who effect robberies of greater magnitude, or burglaries (if free men), are chastised in the same singular manner, after which the tattoo mark of their country is cancelled (consisting simply of having the face cut and gashed in a thousand places), that of another nation substituted, and when partially recovered from the effects of the wounds, the miserable wretches are driven, like beasts, to the sea-coast, and sold into perpetual slavery. *Slaves* guilty of theft, or indeed of almost any other crime, are uniformly decapitated in Yariba, without the benefit of trial; whereas all free men are judged impartially by the elders of the people in the hearing of the king, in the palàver-house, or hall of council.

Yarro, ruler of Khiama, a province of Borghoo, encourages theft, by appropriating part of the stolen property to his own use, which is generally presented to him by the robber in person; but if an individual, after being successful in a depredation, forgets or refuses to tender the accustomed portion of the spoil to his sovereign, he is immediately beheaded, and the whole of his property falls to the king. On my return to that country I was informed by several of the natives, that as soon as their prince heard of our approaching his territories from Yariba, he caused a proclamation to be issued in every town through which we were expected to pass, prohibiting the inhabitants from stealing even a needle from the white men, and threatening with death every one that infringed this law. To this wholesome and timely declaration of Yarro I attribute the great respect in which our persons were held by the multitude, and the reverence with which they regarded our property and effects.

In Yariba and Borghoo, as well as in several other countries, when women find themselves *enceintes*, they must immediately inform their husbands of the circumstance; or in attempt at concealment, are publicly flogged. The same punishment is also inflicted on females who are known to associate with the other sex before the expiration of three years after the birth of an infant, that being the period mothers are obliged to suckle their offspring.

GOVERNMENT.

The government of Badagry, Yariba, Nyffé, and Houssa, is a perfect and unlimited despotism, the sovereigns of those countries exercising absolute power over the lives and property of their subjects, as well as the privilege of enacting the most arbitrary laws, and other acts peculiar to the kingly office. The government of Borghoo, however, partakes more of the nature of a limited monarchy than of real despotism, the people sharing, in some degree, in the management of the state, through the representation of the chiefs or elders of towns, who, like the feudal barons of England in the reign of John, have considerable influence with their sovereign, and are consulted in all affairs of consequence. These chiefs, themselves, are oftentimes factious and turbulent, fomenting innumerable broils and wranglings amongst the people in their respective jurisdictions, to gratify with a better grace their own private feelings of resentment, and to disturb the public peace by arbitrary and unlawful proceedings. The people of Boussa, the principal state in Borghoo, together with those of its sister provinces of Youri, Wow Wow, and Khiama, are indebted to the Bornouese for their origin; or at least the traditions of the natives intimate that Borghoo was colonized from Bornou at a remote era, in which opinion all classes implicitly believe; and, like the Carthaginians of old, the people of the former kingdom are not forgetful of their derivation, but send annually a number of presents by way of acknowledgment to their ancient country; although of late years, owing to the disturbances of the Falatahs, the accustomed presents have not been received in Bornou with the same punctuality as formerly.

AMUSEMENTS.

The recreations of the Africans are few and simple. At Wow Wow horse-racing takes place every Friday, (the Mohammedan Sabbath,) immediately after the compliments of the day are over. The course, which is a mile in length, is kept clean and free from grass, &c. by persons appointed for that purpose by the king; and the race is extremely well contested, exciting amongst the people generally as lively an interest as the same sport does in the minds of my own countrymen. The competitors are oftentimes twelve or fourteen in number, and the rider of the swiftest horse obtains no other reward than the honor of the deed itself, and the privilege of *dancing*, at the conclusion of the

288   AMUSEMENTS.

game, with the king, queens, and princesses of Wow Wow! The inhabitants, on these occasions, attire themselves in their gayest apparel, and, in the evening, assembling in groups in different parts of the town, pass many an hour in singing, dancing, and carousing, till, towards morning, they go tipsy to bed. Horse-racing is, I believe, peculiar to Wow Wow; for in no other African country that I have heard of (except perhaps Khiama), or that came within the reach of my own observation, is a similar amusement preserved. The people of Borghoo divert themselves by playing at a kind of chequers, and throwing cowries from a certain distance into a hole previously dug in the earth; the latter amusement is somewhat similar to our " pitch and toss," and is cultivated by all ranks and both sexes with uncommon ardour. In addition to these pastimes, the higher orders spend whole days in hunting and fishing.

SONGS, MUSIC, &c.

If the character of a nation may be judged of by its Songs, the Africans undoubtedly would be pronounced as the boldest and most martial, as well as the most amorous people, on the face of the globe. Their strains breathe nothing but love and war, and contempt of death; but their conduct, instead of corresponding with such lofty ideas, is the most pusillanimous imaginable, scarcely one amongst them ever evincing a solitary trait of true courage or resolution. Of all figures of speech, they most delight in the use of the "apostrophe;" and it is not uncommon, even but a single day after a defeat, to hear them calling aloud on the names of their absent adversaries, and bestowing upon them all manner of cowardly and reproachful epithets.

" Our enemies tremble and are dismayed when they hear of our approach," sing the people of Yariba; " and at sight of our arrows they die with fear ! See them fleeing like the doe from our fighting men! Behold them falling down and kissing the dust from the feet of our warriors! Haste, haste, Yaribeans! pursue and overtake your enemies; slay them without mercy; stop their voices, that they sing no more at eventide by the light of the moon; they are swift of foot, but they shall not escape you; they are already weary; their journey of life is almost at an end; they have fallen to the earth, and will dance no more. Weep, ye widows of Houssa, and let the lamentations of your children be heard in the land, for they are fatherless, and your husbands have been pierced by the lance of Yariba! They are clothed in darkness, as the noon in a storm. Who can tell whither their spirits are wandering? Weep, ye widows of Houssa; but your tears flow in vain; your husbands will return no more!"

This is the nature of the strains sung by the females of Katunga, (principally the king's wives,) at the celebration of their solemn feasts and festivals: the Houssans (or rather the Falatahs of that country) being their most inveterate enemies, are on all occasions the subject of their poetry, and are made to flee from the Yaribeans in imagination, whilst in reality they are worsted in every engagement. Their social and domestic songs, however, are delivered in recitative, (as are likewise those of the people of Borghoo,) and are the reverse of their public and national ones.

The young females in both kingdoms that may happen to have strong clear voices, are generally selected as wives, or rather concubines, for the ruling monarchs. Their office is principally to attend on the king's person, and sing and fan him to sleep, and the ladies consume great part of the day in these avocations; to vary which they sometimes play music and whistle for a long time together. These ladies also dally with their sovereign, by flinging their arms round his neck, arranging his sable locks with their fingers, playing the fool with his face, and a thousand other fantastic inventions to amuse him, such as the sex know so well how to avail themselves of all over the world. It is the custom in Europe for gentlemen to flatter the graces of the fair sex, whereas in Africa the practice is completely reversed; for the most extravagant encomiums are lavished on the beauty and blandishments of mankind by the gentler part of the creation.

The following imperfect translation of a song, recited by his young wives, to the sovereign of Khiama, may serve as a specimen of the whole of their amatory poetry:—

292   MUSIC.

"Yarrow is fair among men: he shines like a star of the night; who so beautiful as Yarrow? His eyes have greater lustre than the antelope's— more ardour than a young lion's, when he captures his prey. His form is elegant as the palmtree; he is gentle as a kid when she follows her dam. But Yarrow is brave in fight; his enemies tremble at the sound of his name, as a leaf shaken by the wind; they fall to the earth beneath the power of his arm, for he is a mountain of strength. The turtle dove is not so affectionate as our king; doth he not cherish his wives and concubines? Who so lovely as Yarrow? When he is pleased, the moon is not so mild as the light of his countenance; but when he frowns, who shall withstand his wrath? His face lowers like the clouds of heaven in a tempest; O, he is terrible in battle! Awake and be glad, ye daughters of Khiama; sing, ye sons, to the praise of our lord, for he is fair as the morning, and his countenance is like the sun in his strength. He is fair among men; who so beautiful as Yarrow?"

It would be as difficult to detach singing and

dancing from the character of an African, as to change the colour of his skin. I do not think he would live a single week in his own country without participating in these his favourite amusements; to deprive him of which would be indeed worse than death. In every *grade* of society, from the monarch to the meanest slave, he is also fond of instrumental music, even to a passion, and a European fiddler (provided he be not blind,) with no very extraordinary pretensions to excellence in his profession, might travel with ease and comfort, even if he were destitute of a single cowry, from Badagry to Bornou. He would be received every where with open arms, lodged in palaces, and sumptuously fed; although he might, perhaps, feel some trifling inconvenience from excess of kindness, and compulsory detention for a day or two in the principal cities. But, notwithstanding their strong partiality for this kind of music, the instruments of the Africans are of the rudest description. A large drum, made from the trunk of a tree, and covered with sheep-skin; a long brass trumpet, from Barbary; the Arab fiddle, and a kind of dulcimer, formed of bamboo, and played upon with two little sticks, are great favorites in all the interior countries. The people have also guitars, bag-pipes, and tubes of iron, which answer the purpose of tin plates, the sound produced being very similar to the noise of those instruments; but a little flute, like a child's penny whistle in England, is most admired by the Africans; and of all their music this is certainly the most harmonious. Yet even on these instruments they perform most vilely, and produce a horribly discordant noise, which may, perhaps, be delightful to their own ears; but to strangers, if they have the misfortune to be too near the performers, no sounds can be more harsh and disagreeable than such a concert.

Of all the amusements of the Africans, none can equal their song and dance in the still, clear hours of night, when the moon, walking in beauty in the heavens, awakens all the milder affections of their nature, and invites them to gladness and mirth. As soon as this splendid luminary appears above the horizon, every individual, both slave and free, is on the alert,—some to fetch wood from a neighbouring forest, and others to procure provisions in the village; and forming themselves in a circle, generally round a venerable tree, they prepare large fires, in order to frighten away any wild beasts that may be prowling near the spot, and begin their country dance, which does not differ from one extremity of the continent to the other. I have often been a party to these innocent entertainments, which are frequently kept up with inconceivable spirit and agility, till the approach of morning; and as often been delighted with the perfect harmony and kindly feeling that prevailed amongst the dancers. It produces a pleasing and romantic effect, to observe the silvery light of the moon, blending with the radiance of the flames, and thrown upon the sable countenances of the happy group,—as well as the lengthened reflection of the majestic tree cast along the ground, and the moving figures, gliding like shadows across it.

On these occasions all care is completely laid aside, and every one delivers himself up to the dissipation of the moment, without a thought of the morrow, his heart having no *vacuum* for melancholy anticipations. During the intervals of the dance and song, the party either eat and drink, or re-kindle the fires, after which they begin again with renewed ardour. Their songs are composed extempore by one of the party, who recites to his or her companions, and they all join in the strain. They do not contain many poetical beauties, but allude generally to the dancers themselves, to the dread of wild beasts, or commands or entreaties for a particular person to fetch wood. The following, sung in my presence, may serve as a translated specimen of all of them :—

>Come, let us join the dance and song,
>   The moon is bright in heaven ;
>No anxious cares to us belong,
>   To cloud this lovely even.

>The white man midst our festive glee —
>   Forgets his father-land ;
>And the group laughs around our tree
>   By gentle zephyrs fann'd.

HOUSSA SONG.

Haste, Nalla,* to yon forest shade,
    And feed the flickering flame;
How swiftly flies the panting maid
    To earn a deathless name! †

The panther's yell—the lion's roar—
    Resound from wood to wood;
How gladly would they spill our gore!
    How gladly lap our blood!

But we are safe—they dare not come
    To mar our evening sport;
Scared by the fire, or sounding drum,
    They other pleasures court.

Then join the merry dance and song;
    The moon is high in heaven;
No anxious cares to us belong,
    To cloud this lovely even.

When heard at a distance, in the midst of solitary woods, the vocal music of the natives has a pleasing plaintive effect, equalling in softness any I have heard in more civilized countries; and Captain Clapperton and myself used to re-

---

* A female's slave.

† The act of fetching wood in the night season, by reason of the existence of wild beasts in the woods, is considered an enterprize of danger; and those who accept the proposal are greatly eulogised, and held up as examples for others to copy.

main awake in our tent for hours together, listening to its melancholy strains.

It is not to be expected that after these midnight revelries the people are in a condition to rise at a very early hour; indeed the generality of Africans are constitutionally inclined to indolence, a disease which the relaxing nature of their climate by no means tends to lessen; and when not *obliged* to labour, they feel no desire to over-exert themselves, or to shake off their drowsiness, except from a call of necessity. Their soil, in fact, in most parts is so surprisingly rich and productive, as to supersede the necessity of that laborious manual exertion which the cultivation of it requires in many other regions; and in the absence of all intellectual amusements, they dole away the sultry hours of noon in sleeping, lounging about from place to place, gossiping, smoking, or drinking.

SLAVERY.

Slavery, from time immemorial, has flourished in every nation and amongst every people in the interior countries, and seems to be implanted so deeply in the soil, that the slightest hope cannot be entertained of its being speedily outrooted. The slave, however, in most interior districts, is treated with infinitely greater lenity and kindness than among the less civilized natives of the sea coast; and the condition of the slaves of European planters is not to be compared with his, for happiness and comfort. If his character be good, and his honesty unquestioned, the slave of the African is admitted into the house of his master, placed on an equality with himself and male children, thrusts his hand into the same bowl of tuah as they, shares their confidence, and participates in all their pleasures and amusements. An instance is never known of a dependant, having an unblemished character, and active industrious habits, being sent to the coast to be sold; in fact, every one considers this to be the greatest punishment that can be inflicted upon him,—the idea of the whites eating their countrymen, and dyeing their clothes red with their blood, being as general and as deeply-rooted as in the nations through which Mr. Park travelled twenty or thirty years ago. Those sent to the sea-side from the interior are invariably the scum and refuse of the country, — freebooters, lawless refractory fellows, adulterers, and even murderers. Upon the whole, I should consider the situation of the domestic slave of Africa (their relative feelings compared), to be more enviable than that of the household servant of Europe, inasmuch as a feeling of dependence never enters the mind of the former, and, as it has already been observed, he is placed in almost every respect on an equality with his master.

Nature has wisely endowed the African with a bouyant, cheerful, happy temper; so that no calamity, however great, — no grief, however poignant, — is capable of making a deep or lasting impression on his mind. He does indeed display a lively natural feeling when his infant children are snatched forcibly from his embraces, or he himself torn from his home, and kindred, and village-tree, to gaze upon strange faces, and wander amongst foreign scenes; but this emotion is as evanescent as a flash of lightning; he knows no fixed lasting sorrow; past misfortunes are quickly swallowed up in present enjoyment, while anticipations of the future have no power to harass and perplex him, because it is painful for him to think at all, and he does *not* think. I have often seen disobedient slaves, and slaves offered for sale, singing in chains and dancing in fetters, suffering at the same time under a loathsome disease, and an accumulation of misery, the very *thoughts* of which would melt, even to tears, a sympathizing English philanthropist! For their parts, they hardly know what a bitter moment is, and enjoy themselves, although under such apparently overwhelming circumstances, with as keen a zest as if they had been surrounded by their friends and companions, and dancing by the light of the moon, underneath the branches of their favourite tree. In their toilsome journeyings from one part of the country to another, it must be admitted that the *captured* slaves undergo incredible hardships; yet when even they arrive at the end of their march, all their woes are buried for ever in a calabash of *pitto* or *otée*, and they are as merry and thoughtless a day or two afterwards as they ever were.

On the coast, however, things wear a different and far less agreeable aspect; the slaves there are mostly captured from the neighbouring states, and, suddenly losing their darling amusements, become melancholy and pensive on shipboard. The confined, impure air of the vessel augments their sufferings; and when, after landing on an unknown, and to them an unlovely soil, they writhe in agony under the excoriating lash of the unfeeling planter, because they *cannot* work, is it to be marvelled at that, driven to almost desperation, they become morose, unsociable, and headstrong? I have often been a reluctant witness to such disgraceful spectacles, and wondered it was in the power of a human creature to undergo so rigorous a punishment without a murmur.

TIMIDITY OF THE NATIVES.

A vein of *true* courage does not exist, I really believe, in any individual of the nations we visited. In most savage and half-civilized countries, such as the Tonga Islands, and the rarely frequented districts of North America, for instance, sparks of noble resolution and greatness of soul are oftentimes observable in the natives: but the timidity of the African character is every where apparent. The eyes of the Gooberites, as well as those of the people of Borghoo, not unfrequently flash with a wild expression of ferocity, and their actions sometimes correspond with this indication of a barbarous nature, but it is not *courage*, and gradually fades at the approach of real danger. The people rarely make an attack on each other, or on a common enemy, excepting when they have a decided superiority of numbers, or are placed under circumstances peculiarly favourable to their operations; and even when this is the case, they are more mindful of individual safety than the general welfare, trusting rather to their heels than their arms to make good their retreat, if the least danger threatens them. They have no tradition of a chief amongst them that possessed, when living, a calm, unshrinking, persevering spirit; their greatest leaders now (as in former years) being all of one stamp, revengeful and passionate in war, and if not successful on the first onset, like the lion, making rarely a second spring. The Falatahs, who claim all the bravery to themselves, are to a man dastardly poltroons, and have met with their astonishing good fortune,—not by open, manly courage, but by treachery, deceit, and cunning — by imposing on the superstitious fears of the simple aborigines, and by artfully insinuating themselves into the good opinion of the very people it was their secret intention to enslave, and, like the adder in the fable, watching the opportunity to bite the hand that nourished them. It would not be well to say that they have greater positive courage than the negro, but they have less pusillanimity and more shrewdness than he. Not all the glowing pleasures after death, which the religion of the Falatah teaches him to expect — not the unshaken belief in predestination that prompts the gloomy and enthusiastic Turk to rush headlong upon his fate —not the promised enjoyment for ever of the seventy-two lovely *houris* awarded to those that fall in the cause of Mohammed—not even the fearful and tremendous war-cry of his countrymen, " Allah Ackbar ! " (God is victorious !) has the power of arousing the energies of the Falatah, or inspiring him with ardour and impetuosity in the fight. Securely shielded, as he fancies himself to be, from the effects of the arrows and spears of his adversary, by wearing thickly-quilted armour, and fortifying himself with Arab charms, the Falatah may indeed exhibit an air of defiance for a time; but if any thing occurs to stagger his faith in the virtue of his ægis, off he scampers, without considering the example he sets his companions, and does not stop till he is far beyond the reach of even imaginary danger!

THE ARTS, &c.

Of the imitative arts, painting and sculpture, the Falatah understands absolutely nothing; indeed, the former art is almost entirely unknown in the interior, whilst the latter, however, is practised amongst the natives of Jannah, Yariba, and Borghoo, who have a natural fondness for it, and produce various specimens that evince considerable skill in the artist. Figures of men, as well as those of snakes, crocodiles, &c. are carved in bas-relief by them; and, contrasting the rudeness of the instruments used, with the fineness and delicacy of some of the indentions, it excites one's admiration for their persevering industry and ingenious labours. The people are acquainted with many of the useful arts, such as working in iron, tanning, dyeing, &c. The smiths are surprisingly skilful in their profession, and fuse and fashion iron into all manner of forms with extraordinary ease and dispatch. Hundreds of these useful artizans are scattered over the country, and Nyffé in particular swarms with them; they are universally respected, and treated with the utmost deference by every rank.

The variety of the dyes of the Africans has been often remarked, and the richness and beauty which they maintain, notwithstanding constant exposure to the elements, elicit the admiration of even Europeans. The exquisite colour of native cottons, in particular, is unrivalled; and the art of dyeing is carried to as great a height of perfection in many countries in the interior as in the more enlightened portions of the world. The art of tanning is also carried on with equal spirit and success; and the leather dressed by the natives is equal, if not superior, to that manufactured in England. Saddlers, shoemakers, and tailors, are to be met with in most nations in Africa, and for ingenuity in their respective trades, yield to few.

A smithy in Nyffé, &c. is very similar to that which has been described in the celebrated narrative of Mr. Park's first journey into the interior of Africa. The process of the fusion and fashioning of iron is exceedingly simple; and notwithstanding the very few tools that are used by working smiths, their quickness and ingenuity cannot be excelled, even by a European professing the same trade, and who has the advantages afforded by an acquaintance with all the rules of art.

DRY AND WET SEASONS, &C.

The air, especially in the dry season, is oppressively hot; and if a mist or haze that sometimes hangs between the earth and sky, did not intercept the sun's rays, it would be wholly insupportable. The African sky seldom displays the clear, rich ether, or the beautiful and evanescent touches of the Italian; but if the appearance of the heavens be less lovely to the sight in the former country, by the existence of vapoury clouds in the air, the heat is rendered infinitely more tolerable by the same cause. Towards the latter part of the dry season, and all nature seems parched while withering (except on the margins of rivers), the earth is literally baked as hard as flint, while the birds and beasts, fluttering and panting in the shades, by their cries and moans seem to bewail the absence of rain. But no sooner does the wet season set in, than vegetation suddenly springing up, bursts into being; a fresh and redundant luxuriance of life breathes and floats around; the hills and dales are covered with a delightful verdure; the earth, the air, the sky, seem smiling in joy, and refreshed into gladness and beauty. Every thing looks cheerful and attractive: the horned cattle gambol on the plains, and the sheep and goats frisk on the slopes of mountains and hills; man himself appears animated with a new existence; pleasure swells in his veins, and dances on his countenance, and he enters cordially into the enjoyment which every province of nature invites him to partake in common with itself. This is generally during the intervals of the showers; it rather *floods* than *rains* in Africa, and continues without intermission for the space of twelve hours, when it suddenly stops, and a cessation of rain for twenty-four hours not unfrequently takes place.

The sun setting in Africa is a grand and magnificent object; he then appears shorn of his beams, and may be gazed at by the naked eye for any length of time, without our experiencing a single painful sensation in that delicate organ. When he sinks below the horizon, he looks like a huge sphere of burning gold, and the hills (if any) towards the west seem as if on fire by the vivid reflection of his rays. Twilight is of short duration, and if the moon does not shine, darkness soon covers the earth like a veil. In no other country have I seen such cloudless, lovely nights, or so mildly beautiful a moon. I do not wonder that the natives sometimes adore her;

she possesses a soothing, softening influence, of which they themselves are susceptible; and there is certainly something more captivating in the delightful appearance of so resplendent an orb, sailing gracefully through the purple vault of heaven, than in the figures of disgusting reptiles and monsters which the natives so often worship.

END OF VOL. I.

J. B. NICHOLS AND SON,
25, Parliament Street.

www.ingramcontent.com/pod-product-compliance
Lightning Source LLC
Chambersburg PA
CBHW032332230426
43664CB00039B/94